Finding Joy

ONE WOMAN'S JOURNEY BACK TO FAITH

Joy Wooderson

ISBN: 1-4392-5255-6
ISBN-13: 9781439252550

Visit www.booksurge.com to order additional copies.

In grateful memory of my friend and spiritual mentor

Joan P. Almand

who consistently pointed me in the right direction—
toward a loving, trustworthy God.

The Equal-Arm Balance Model

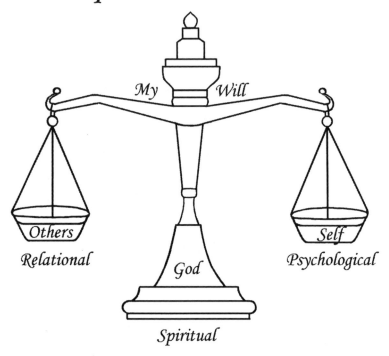

*Love the LORD your God with all your heart and
with all your soul and with all your mind. [. . .]
Love your neighbor as yourself.
Matthew 22:37, 39*

Contents

A Note from the Author vii

Acknowledgements.................................ix

Part One – Weighted Down

1. I Wonder ...? 3
2. All Alone 13
3. "Did God *Really* Say ...?".........................27

Part Two – Shaky Props

4. The Faith of My Father(s) 39
5. Two Different Worlds Merge.......................57
6. Forming Ideas About God.........................69
7. Shoulds and Oughts 85

Part Three – The Master Designer's Blueprint

8. Back to Basics 99
9. The Equal-Arm Balance Model 113

Part Four – The Support Column: God

10. God Above and Around Me.....................125
11. God Next To Me 137
12. God In Me?....................................147

PART FIVE — THE CROSSBAR: HUMAN WILL

13. It's My Choice 157
14. Testing the Theory. 171
15. Solitude and Silence. 187
16. Learning to Trust an Invisible God Is Hard. 195
17. The Church: Conduit or Obstacle? 211

PART SIX — THE SUSPENDED PAN OF *OTHERS*

18. Wisdom School. 227
19. *Others'* Expectations of Me. .239
20. My Expectations of *Others* 247

PART SEVEN — THE SUSPENDED PAN OF *SELF*

21. Defining *Self* 259
22. Two *Selfs*? 273
23. A New Perspective. 283

PART EIGHT — ADJUSTING THE WEIGHTS

24. A Winding, Arduous, Battle-Filled Path. 295
25. "The Greatest Counselor" 307
26. Training … and More Training 321
27. The Ultimate Crisis. 337

PART NINE — LIFE IN BALANCE

28. An Integrating Force. 349
29. A Revised Concept of God 363
30. Finding Joy. 375

References. 385

A Note From the Author ...

Dear Reader,

I am honored you have chosen to join me on my journey. I pray you will gain spiritual insight through my search for authentic faith from within the context of the religious world.

My story spans a century. I will show you, from my own experience, how a religious heritage can be formed, practiced, and passed on through succeeding generations, often without question.

As a mature adult, I found myself in a crisis of faith, tempted to discard my inherited Christian beliefs. However, I could not shake the suspicion that something worthwhile lay buried under the trappings of organized, denominational Christianity. This curiosity sent me off on a quest to re-examine my clergy grandparents' and parents' beliefs. I sifted through the core doctrines of the Christian faith, relegated some man-made interpretations to a peripheral position, and ultimately discovered the reality of a personal relationship with the living, loving, invisible God.

The late Joan Almand played a significant role in guiding me out of my confusion and doubt by consistently pointing me in the right direction. Some of her pearls of wisdom, what I have dubbed "Joanisms," are reflected in my story. I have also offered my own "Pointers" at the end of each chapter, plus a blank page on which to record your reflections, if you wish. May my story spark your interest in taking a fresh look at the timeless, enduring, relevant Christian faith, and by doing so help shed light on your own spiritual path.

Journey with me now on the often harrowing, sometimes exciting, always uncertain path that leads from religious bondage to the freedom of a relationship with the invisible God.

Your fellow traveler,

Joy Wooderson
O'Fallon, Missouri
www.joywooderson.com

Acknowledgements

A late bloomer in the field of writing creative nonfiction, I had a lot to learn about the craft as I embarked on this project. Many people contributed to my writing education, and I would like to mention those individuals and groups who made a significant difference.

Michael Steinberg and Jocelyn Bartkevicius opened my mind to the art of memoir at the 2005 Eckerd College "Writers in Paradise" workshop.

Monthly meetings and excellent speakers at Saturday Writers, a sub-chapter of the Missouri Writers' Guild, expanded my base of knowledge.

Weekly critique sessions with the talented writers of the Scribes' Tribe in O'Fallon, Missouri, polished my work and alerted me to pitfalls. I owe a huge debt of gratitude to the primary members of this group: Amy Harke-Moore, Candace Carrabus Rice, Tricia L. Sanders, Doyle Suit, Jerrel Swingle, and Tom Carpenter for their willingness to share their expertise and their unflagging support.

Special thanks to the folks who generously gave their time as manuscript readers: John Witkowski in Georgia; Margaret Madden, Anne-Marie Sullivan, and

Judy Swingle in Missouri. Emily Moore took my line scratchings and turned them into a comprehensible image.

God went to extraordinary lengths to connect me to my capable editor, Amy Harke-Moore. He knew just the right person who could prayerfully and carefully guide me through the creative process.

Lastly, my dear friend and encourager, Jacquelyn Ehrlich, played a key role in instigating my move from Atlanta to St. Louis—on which everything else related to publication of this book hinged.

To all, you have my deepest gratitude.

PART ONE

WEIGHTED DOWN

1

I WONDER ...?

*Man's heart strives after unending eternal happiness.
Thou hast created us, O Lord, for Thyself, and our heart is
restless until it rests in Thee.*

—St. Augustine

My lungs at bursting point, I flopped on the stone ledge, propped my back against the wall, and stretched my aching legs. The pounding in my ears subsided as my brain told my heart it could ease up now. I'd made it! I was at the top of Mount Sinai.

Inhaling the dry, clear air, I settled myself more comfortably as my eyes scanned the magnificent view. Range upon range of rosy granite mountains towered over parched riverbeds that waited expectantly to carry spring rains to thirsty plains. It was an inhospitable land, where those who struggled to survive the terrain clustered with their camels and goats around intermittent oases.

I had joined a tour group traveling to Egypt, Jordan, the Sinai Peninsula, and Israel. Love of travel lurked in my genes, passed down by my seafaring English great-grandfather who regularly crossed the Atlantic as first mate of one of those early combination steam/sailing ships. On every trip, I liked to form a visual image of the world map and plot my journey. The dot of my home in Atlanta, Georgia, was a long way from the ledge on Mount Sinai.

The mystery of ancient Egypt had beckoned for years, so I jumped at the chance of an adventure. When the tour leader instructed us to purchase a water bottle strapped to a belt and to pack a flashlight, hat, and pharmaceutical items to counter King Tut's Revenge, I knew I wasn't heading for the typical beach vacation.

In addition to experiencing the grandeur of this ancient civilization, the trip would bring to life one of my favorite Bible stories—the Exodus. That amazing escape of the Hebrew slaves from Egypt and their journey through the Sinai desert to Canaan, the land God had promised them. I would walk in the footsteps of Moses and the Israelites. Reality would replace imagination—imagination fueled by Cecil B. DeMille's magnificent portrayal of this historic event in the movie *The Ten Commandments.*

From the moment I set foot in Cairo, the timelessness of Egypt overwhelmed me. Five thousand years of civilization slipped away as I stood in the shadow of the Great Pyramid of Cheops at Giza. The wonder of this complex and enigmatic tomb mystified archaeologists, architects, and engineers.

The world had changed so much through the centuries. I lived in the era of men walking on the moon, satellite communications, and astounding medical and technological advances. Yet, it appeared little had changed in Egypt from the time of the Pharaohs. Along the banks of a dirty canal, an old man formed bricks with mud and straw and set them out to dry like the Hebrew slaves did. The Nile was still the Nile, and sailboats known as *feluccas* continually plied their way from shore to shore. Obelisks and temple columns guarded their secrets while towering over tourists.

The opulence and grandeur of that era came alive as the tour guide translated the meaning of the hieroglyphics. Imagination transported me to the time of a tyrannical Pharaoh, a nation of ill-treated Hebrew slaves, and the shepherd whose God, Yahweh, told him to lead the people to freedom. I could almost hear the tap of sandaled feet, the swish of garments and fans as merchants and citizens bustled about their business. The slaves who built the cities and temples for the glory of Egypt faced grinding toil and hardship, with only death holding hope for escape.

The mood of another age lingered as we continued via Jordan into the Sinai Peninsula. Geographically, this was a triangular area bounded by the Gulf of Suez and the Gulf of Aqaba. The Book of Exodus described how Yahweh (God) led the Hebrews on foot, with their herds and possessions, out of Egypt into the wilderness. We had the luxury of a tour bus. For mile after mile we bounced our way along the "road" that was nothing more than a dry riverbed, the wheels churning up choking clouds of dust. I couldn't decide which was worse—suffocating under the scarf over my nose and mouth, which gave the illusion of filtering out the dust, or recklessly gasping air and hoping my lungs would one day become unclogged. To the curious bystanders, we must have looked like a busload of bandits. After an interminable ride, we arrived dusty, tired, and sore at The Monastery of St. Catherine where we were to spend the night. Ahead of us lay the adventure of climbing Mount Sinai at dawn.

Although historians and archaeologists are unable to pinpoint which mountain was designated as the "mountain of God" in Exodus, the general consensus holds the most likely candidate as being Jebel Musa, Arabic for "Mountain of Moses." The mountain looms over the desert in striking contrast to its surroundings. At its foot nestles the monastery, constructed on the site of a church built by the Roman Emperor Constantine nearly 1,600 years ago. European artisans spent almost twenty years sculpting its ornate basilica, chapel, and library. The monastery owes its existence to a wild desert plant that grows in its ancient courtyard, which the local monks believe is the living remnant of the original burning bush that attracted Moses' attention. Defying the desert's eternal heat and dust, the monastery stands in isolation, a tangible memorial to one of the most significant events in Judeo-Christian history.

The hospitable monks provided a simple meal and camp cots. To our weary bodies, those unyielding camp cots felt like down mattresses.

At 4:30 a.m., flashlights in hand, water bottles dangling at our waists, we set forth into the cool, early morning air. The path snaking up the side of the mountain became visible as darkness gave way to the first light of dawn. We paused to watch the sun peep out between the stark mountains. Its warmth rapidly overtook the coolness, ushering in another scorching day in the desert.

The path steepened, the temperature soared, and my dangling water bottle no longer seemed an encumbrance. What I thought would be a breeze to my reasonably fit thirty-seven-year-old body became a challenge. Only the recognition of this once-in-a-lifetime opportunity kept one foot in front of the other. Red faced and panting, I reached the summit and sank onto the stone ledge.

The voices of my fellow tourists murmured around me, yet I felt isolated. Thousands of years of history oozed from the cold granite of this mountain range. A million life stories had been absorbed into the sandy river beds. I felt as insignificant as a pebble, content to rest quietly.

My thoughts drifted to the story of Moses and the Exodus. The Hebrew slaves traveled from the security and bondage of Egypt into the uncertainty and freedom of this desert. I imagined them in a sprawling camp around the base of the mountain—people, tents, goats, sheep, and camels everywhere—as the smoke of a thousand fires drifted skyward.

What were their hopes as they embarked on their journey? What did they expect from Moses and the invisible God who, after four hundred years of silence, had now decided to intervene in their plight?

Time and again, the Bible says Yahweh met with Moses on a mountain such as this. The Exodus account described an open, honest relationship between them. Moses told God He had made a huge mistake in choosing him to lead the Hebrews to freedom. He pointed out his dubious past (Prince of Egypt turned murderer and fugitive) and lack of communication skills (forty years of talking to sheep does not make a man a compelling orator). Moses recommended God pick someone else.

At God's insistence, Moses agreed to the task. Becoming the liaison between Yahweh and the Hebrews did not turn him into a "yes" man. He complained when things got difficult. He expressed his frustration with Yahweh and the stubborn people. He obeyed Yahweh's orders while sometimes interjecting his own opinion. Living interaction forged a relationship. Moses became an exception in the history of God's dealings with humans. Prior to this, God had only spoken through a prophet via vision or dream. Now He honored Moses by speaking directly to him. Moses actually saw the form of God, although not His face. As the story unfolded, their relationship developed to the point where God entrusted Moses with His Law, the Ten Commandments.

How wonderful it would be to have that kind of unhindered, one-on-one relationship with my Creator, I mused. Yet, was it realistic to hope that I, or anyone, could build a relationship with God in this modern age? Perhaps the type of relationship Moses had was only for his time?

My inner life was an inexplicable mess. I had started out with high hopes, only to have them dashed on the rocks of disillusionment and confusion. I professed to be a Christian, but my heart resembled the dry, dusty desert below. Over the years, religious traditions, theological confusion, and emotional trauma had been piled on me, like blankets on someone in bed, until I suffocated under rules, restrictions, and codes of behavior. I felt as trapped as a convict in a prison, or as a Hebrew slave dominated by an Egyptian taskmaster. Disappointed and resentful, I felt God had not given me what I wanted most—a Knight in Shining Armor, someone to sweep me up into happiness. Surely my painstaking efforts to please Him deserved some reward? My parents' faith seemed to work for them, but it hadn't done much for me.

The gouges of painful interactions with church organizations and professing Christians quivered deep inside me. Life had become a never-ending struggle to measure up to others' expectations while hiding the aching emptiness inside. The effort resulted in discouragement and disheartenment.

The call for a group picture broke my reverie. A tiny church formed the backdrop, and then we began the descent to the monastery—infinitely worse than the ascent. Approximately 3,000 large steps led straight down the back of the mountain. I will never forget the ache and stiffness resulting from that exertion.

Our next stop was Jerusalem and its surroundings. At last I could visualize the setting for all those childhood Bible stories: the rolling hills around Bethlehem where Jesus was born, the often destroyed walls encircling the old city, the road that wound its way to Bethany. I stood among the olive trees in the Garden of Gethsemane, mused at the site of Solomon's and Herod's temples, and floated across the Sea of Galilee to Capernaum.

Numerous shrines and holy places beckoned me inside.

It was wonderful, it was inspiring, and it did nothing to assuage my gnawing dissatisfaction. The openness of the desert and the perception of an unhindered connection with God contrasted starkly to the formalities and rituals of organized religion. A longing to throw off the suffocating trappings stirred within, like a faint breath of fresh air in a stale room, as though my idle wondering had opened a window in my mind. For the first time I acknowledged my religion as being deficient. Contrary to what I had been taught, it did not meet my deepest needs. I needed something more; I needed a faith that worked!

Sometimes we think that reaching out to God requires determined effort or a dedicated act of will, followed by some emotional expression. For me it started with a wistful, simple, "I wonder . . .?" wrung from a hurting heart in the middle of the Sinai Desert.

POINTER: Begin by Opening a Window in Your Mind

- Have you found modern Christianity disappointing? If so, what events or circumstances triggered your disappointment?

- Are you confused by differing interpretations of religious beliefs?

- Are you suffering under the trappings of organized religion—the formalities, codes of behavior, and dictates?

- Perhaps you've never considered trying to get to know the God of Christianity? Why not open your mind to the possibility this might be worth exploring?

POINTER REFLECTIONS:

2

ALL ALONE

The mood of living in a bygone era faded as I picked up the threads of life in Atlanta. Yet, surprisingly, a small part of me lingered in the Sinai. The experience had crystallized my longing for freedom and created an image that gave shape to vague feelings. My curiosity had been aroused.

But the pace of modern life didn't allow the luxury of prolonged introspection, and daily routine soon took precedence over any wisps of memory. There was no noticeable effect from my mountaintop musings; no miraculous transformation took place.

It had been six years since I emigrated from South Africa, the fascinating, complex land of my birth—a country rich in history and cultural diversity, a land of stark contrasts. Few places in the world so vividly illustrate the precarious balance of nature. It's a magical land, where the natural entertainment never ceases, where the air itself is imbued with the mystique of Africa. Day turns into night, like someone switching off a light, and blackness descends.

While love of my beautiful country ran deep and strong, my life there fell far short of expectations. I was deeply disappointed over not being married. Further, being the daughter of a prominent clergyman added an unwelcome layer of complexity to my life. Nevertheless, I had tried to build a tolerable existence. In many ways it resembled living in a deep rut—confining, but safe. The surrounding walls of warm dirt allowed my anesthetized emotions to lie undisturbed, detached from the throb and pulse outside.

In 1970 my parents decided to retire. Dad had devoted almost forty years of his life to the church founded by my grandparents in 1924 and was well known in the city and throughout the country. He had established five satellite churches in the districts around Durban and had built twenty-seven African churches through the mission conferences he spearheaded. Mom and Dad's combined ministry had touched thousands of lives. Dad felt he should leave the city in fairness to his successor, and they were drawn to the United States.

Feelings of dismay at the prospect of uprooting myself washed over me like the waves off the beach in Durban. My younger sister Claudia, my only sibling, had attended college in the U.S. She had already made the decision to return to America to teach and ultimately pursue her education. I was faced with the choice of joining my immediate family overseas or remaining alone in South Africa. Neither prospect appealed to me. Living by myself in an apartment was the last thing I wanted, to say nothing of the upheaval and challenge of starting again in a strange country. Yet, remaining alone in South Africa raised the specter of even greater distress, separation from close family members by a vast ocean. So I threw my mind into preparations for the big move and ignored my dragging emotional feet.

Mom and Dad left, and I waited for Mom to petition for my Permanent Resident visa once she arrived in the U.S. Being single, I was put on "Immediate Relative" status, and my approval came through within two months. With a last look at the magnificent African sunset, I boarded the plane in Johannesburg. Two suitcases contained all my worldly possessions; two boxes of beloved books would catch up with me later.

If only I could have lost the crate of emotional baggage that insisted on following me!

Those first few years were a mix of misery and wonder. It takes enthusiasm, energy, and determination to build a new life in a strange country, and I lacked all three. My move was a result of my parents' decision rather than my own, and my emotional feet still dragged.

I arrived in the U.S. convinced my unhappiness and the hurt I had suffered were directly attributable to "the church." My parents' total absorption with service to God and the congregation had damaged me. I didn't exactly blame God for not intervening, but I questioned His lack of involvement in my life.

My first temp job in Atlanta confirmed my dire circumstances. The agency sent me to a small office as receptionist. It was a nightmare. The Southern dialect could have been Romanian, and my own distinctly different accent didn't help communication. I seemed to spend my day saying "Pardon! Pardon me! Could you repeat that?" My boss stared long and hard at one phone slip indicating a call from Mr. Baile, trying to identify the caller. We laughingly determined the name was "Bell"—with a Southern pronunciation.

After my parents arrived in the U.S., friends urged them to continue their ministry activities rather than retire by a lake in Tennessee. Dad was sixty-six, Mom sixty, and each enjoyed vigorous health. They purchased a double-wide mobile home, parked it on private property, and settled a few miles from my apartment.

Mom and I relied heavily on each other for companionship. Much of this was due to being transplants in a new country, having left former friends and family. The comfort of familiarity drew me like a magnet to all Mom represented. The old wall clock, which had been a wedding present, still chimed loudly every quarter hour, only now it lived in the breakfast area in Atlanta instead of the dining room in Durban. The beautiful oil painting by South African artist Gabriel de Jongh hung above the television. For a short while I could find respite in the cocoon of stability and security of "home."

Mom's sense of humor provided built-in entertainment. Obstinate, unpredictable, determined, indomitable, I never knew quite what to expect. No amount of reasoning ever dissuaded her from her opinion that global warming was caused by some fiendish Russian plot. She was a woman of conviction—logical and illogical. Our conversations over cups of tea revolved around safe topics: the garden and home, church activities, theological questions, family news, or current events. My compartmentalized emotions allowed me to function at a superficial level without revealing the gnawing pain within. Mom's solution to my mood swings was a delicious home-cooked meal. Anything on a deeper level was ignored, or at least overlooked. She turned to prayer when faced with complex situations, not talking.

My life improved as I met more people and became involved in social activities. Several fellows in the church singles group looked promising, generating moments of mild infatuation. I was now in my mid-thirties. My marriage prospects dimmed with each passing year. Desperation hovered, so I turned up the fervency level of my prayers. I wanted God's best and was unwilling—or scared—to take matters into my own hands. I waited and prayed. And nobody came on the scene.

In 1973 the pastor of the Pentecostal church I attended offered me an administrative position. I wasn't thrilled about working at a church, especially one where my father served on staff, but I accepted. More money held the lure of an air-conditioned car, more clothes.

Good things came out of my time at the church. The senior minister detected latent talent and offered me an exciting opportunity—assisting him writing high school level Sunday School curriculum. I discovered creativity within myself, a source of enjoyment and satisfaction. While my mind expanded, my emotions stagnated behind their protective shell.

My colleague on the writing project was Joan Almand, who would in time become one of the most important people in my life. Poor Joan. She thought she would have to get a two-by-four to smash through my fortress-like emotional walls. Instead, she used acceptance and caring interest until a crack appeared. Twelve years older and single mother of five, Joan became my mentor. She was the first person to demonstrate a desire to know the hidden Joy, the real person.

To the casual observer, I adjusted well to building a new life in Georgia. They saw an intelligent, reasonably attractive, capable young woman with a certain uniqueness and a very odd accent. The real Joy struggled through every day, battling to fit in. Recurring questions plagued my mind: *Why, God? Why am I so unhappy?* Like a wound that continually festers, the hurt at the core of my being nagged that something was amiss. Had I missed out on finding "God's perfect will" for my life, the center of which supposedly held peace and happiness?

I finally latched onto an idea that took the pressure off me and fit neatly into my understanding of "God's will." In reality, I formulated a one-sided bargain with God.

It's My Calling

I came to the conclusion it was my "calling" to devote myself to Mom and Dad. They were aging, esteemed "servants of the Lord" who had dedicated their lives to God and ministry. It was my duty as a good daughter to keep an eye on them, then, when they were gone, God would surely reward my selflessness by giving me the wonderful person I so richly deserved. There was no way He would leave me alone in the world—He was not that unkind. So I rationalized my situation and justified clinging to my parents. It was much easier to think this way than risk looking deeply within myself, at my relationship with them, or at my preconceived ideas about God and His ways.

Externally, I demonstrated the behavior of a good Christian. Sincere in my beliefs, I knew the language of Christians and could converse easily. To my parents I was a model daughter, attentive and caring.

Only in the quietness of my home did I acknowledge the nagging disappointment, the feeling of having missed out on the important relationships in life. An underlying restlessness exploded when I was forced to spend too much time alone. So I filled my days with a multitude of distractions—family activities, church involvement, travel, and superficial friendships. My work represented the only aspect of my life over which I exerted a measure of control, and climbing the corporate ladder became the focus of my energies.

My visits with my mother acted as a salve to my troubled heart. This was one place I could show up at any time and be welcomed—and fed. Their delightful property showed the results of the hard work of two ardent English gardeners. Mom's indomitable spirit kicked in, and she produced magnificent roses grown in red Georgia clay.

Every once in a while my mind drifted back to the Sinai. I still longed for a relationship with God, but my deepest yearning centered on someone to fill the void in my heart. I continued to attend church regularly— now Baptist—as I had no intention of jeopardizing any possibility that God would send Mr. Right my way by staying away from church. My pastor, a seasoned Bible teacher, spoke about the positives of the Christian life and all that God wanted to provide for His children.

This only intensified my confusion. God had graciously helped me through the difficult, early years of adjustment to life in the U.S.A. I traced His overruling hand in my circumstances.

Crash!

On a cold January day in 1985, my shaky emotional props collapsed. Mom died of a heart attack. I lost the companionship and support of the most important person in my life.

Somehow I functioned during those dark years, working full time at a demanding job, looking after my aging father, and maintaining both our homes. And the unhappiness that began as a clinging spider-web turned into a shroud, binding my heart and mind.

My thoughts bounced backwards and forwards like a tennis ball as I weighed the good things God had given me against the one major thing He hadn't and struggled to reconcile the two. If God were kind, why didn't He give me what I considered a good gift? The desire for a mate was perfectly normal. In fact, a scripture supported my reasoning: "No good thing does he withhold from those whose walk is blameless."[1] I wasn't perfect by any means, but I certainly warranted an "A" for effort.

Couples told how God had "miraculously" engineered circumstances to bring them together. An all-powerful, all-knowing God could do whatever He pleased. Either He was ignoring me, or He deliberately chose not to respond to my request. I felt slighted—and resentful.

Each Sunday morning I slipped quietly into a seat in the balcony of the sanctuary. I smiled at the folks around me, sang enthusiastically, and took notes on the sermon in order to apply what was being taught. People saw a well-dressed, forty-something woman who attended alone. Nobody noticed the pain behind the smile or the tears that flowed with the hymns "Jesus, Lover of my Soul" or "Rock of Ages."

I committed to setting my alarm clock thirty minutes earlier in order to spend time reading my Bible in search of answers. *Streams in the Desert*, a compilation of scripture, poems, and devotional writings by Mrs. Charles E. Cowman, became my spiritual lifeline. Day after day I read, until the pages of my book grew tattered.

Like a drowning person clutching at a passing log, I clung to the words found in Psalm 27: "I would have despaired unless I had believed that I would see the goodness of the LORD in the land of the living."[2] It didn't change anything, but it offered hope. One day the pain would end. One day things would be better.

Three years after my mother died, the phone rang early one morning. It was Dad telling me he had chest pain. The paramedics recommended I take him to the hospital because of his past history of heart problems. For two days his life hung in the balance, until the doctor told us he would not pull through. The hours passed agonizingly slowly as my sister and I watched his pulse rate fall on the monitor.

In the wee hours, he stirred. In a clear, surprisingly strong voice he quoted three scriptures, one after the other:

The LORD bless thee, and keep thee: The LORD make his face shine upon thee, and be gracious unto thee: The LORD lift up his countenance upon thee, and give thee peace.[3]

Trust in the LORD with all thine heart; and lean not unto thine own understanding. In all thy ways acknowledge him, and he shall direct thy paths.[4]

Not by might, nor by power, but by my Spirit, saith the LORD of hosts.[5]

With tears running down our faces, Claudia and I quoted the words along with Dad. After adding a few "Hallelujahs," he fell silent. A few hours later his life slipped quietly away.

Dad had pronounced his final benediction on a congregation of two—his daughters. He reemphasized truths he passionately believed.

My Hot Line to Heaven Has Been Disconnected

Those who still have a parent living cannot fully appreciate what happens when the realization hits for the first time that you're an orphan. For me, there was an added dimension to the loss. Dad's limited resources meant he was never my financial safety net. However, I could call on him to pray for any particular need—and God heard Dad's prayers.

An incorrigible optimist, he searched leaden skies, spied a minute patch of blue, and announced with

enthusiasm that the weather was clearing. His temperament was such that he looked for the best in people and
believed the best of them. Consequently, when he applied his natural optimism to the realm of Christianity
and the practical application of God's Word, he became
a very positive influence on all around him. He had a
simple, childlike trust in a good God.

"Don't worry, dear. The Lord will sort it out."

"But, Dad," I'd protest. "It's not as simple as that!"

All the "But, Dad's" in the world didn't phase him.
He knew what he believed. He had proved the faithfulness and goodness of God, and that was enough.

Now my hot line to heaven had been disconnected.
I felt more alone than ever.

I acknowledged how God had woven His continuing
care and protection like a red thread into the tapestry
of my experiences. Nevertheless, I couldn't understand
why my course was so unlike everyone else's. I looked
around at people I knew. What different paths their lives
had taken. My contemporaries had grown children and
were enjoying, or anticipating enjoying, grandchildren.
Many of them had beautiful homes and financial security. They were entering a new phase of their marital
relationship as time and money afforded opportunities
for travel and pleasure.

Surely now God would graciously intervene on my
behalf and give me the desire of my heart? After all the
heartache of past years, I deserved some happiness and
personal fulfillment.

It was time for JOY—the person and the emotion!

POINTER: Reflect, Contemplate, Meditate

Allow your mind to drift quietly over past years.

- What circumstances brought you to where you are now?

- Which people played major roles in your life?

- Have you ever felt God was deaf to your prayers or pleading?

- That He let you down?

- During times of crisis, when waves of trouble and disappointment crash over you, who represents your lifeline? Why?

POINTER REFLECTIONS:

3

"DID GOD *REALLY* SAY ... ?"

The first response of our lives to God is the act of faith. Until we abandon ourselves to that, nothing else will make sense.
—Eugene Peterson

Things were looking up—I had a man in my life! Not just any man, but one I'd known for many years, a good friend. No doubt he was the answer to my prayers. God had done what I thought He might do, given me a reward for my devotion and care of my parents. I would not spend the rest of my days alone. What a relief! Sure, I faced making huge adjustments, but I would certainly give the relationship my best efforts, working hard to make him happy. We had fun times together—and in group activities. After carrying heavy responsibility for so many years and making major decisions on my own, I liked having a man take a leadership role.

Months passed, and I grudgingly acknowledged the sick feeling lodged in my stomach was trying to tell me something—the friendship had stalled. Once again I watched my dreams evaporate and my optimism dissipate. The weepin' and wailin' of country music about unrequited love matched my mood. God had let me down again.

Finally, the dam wall I had erected to contain my emotions cracked. I found myself staring morosely at the face in the mirror. Eyes dulled with disappointment and disillusionment gazed back at me. If eyes were the window to the soul, this soul was in a sorry state. I saw a shell of a person, with nothing on the inside. My entire life had been spent trying to please God, my parents, the church people, my family.

What I always feared had happened to me. I had reached mid-life with no spouse, children, or grandchildren, no parents, not even a brother-in-law, niece, or nephew. My sister lived miles away. My job no longer satisfied. God had not given me someone to fill the void in my heart, and my deep unhappiness took its toll on my health and mental well-being.

Spiritually, I lived on fumes. Nothing I tried replenished my resources. The Deceiver, Satan, came at me in the way he did with Eve so long ago in the Garden of Eden, with the same subtle, rational question "Did God *really* say . . . ?" Supposing I had been misled all my life? My parents' faith seemed to work for them, but it wasn't doing much for me. My earnest striving to follow God and do His will had landed me in a mess.

Further, other voices that had a different understanding of Christianity—a more humanistic approach—clamored for attention. *Maybe I should leave my church, since how did I know what I was being taught was Truth? Had my pastor pumped me full of stuff about trusting God when it didn't work the way he said? Were all those promises I had tried to claim as my own merely a "carrot on a stick?"* Doubts plagued my mind.

Dempsey, the cynical cop in the British television drama *Dempsey and Makepiece,* summed up what I was beginning to believe, "Life is hard, and then you die!" Was religion really the opiate of the people, as Karl Marx stated, a means of anesthetizing the pain of living or a crutch for those who couldn't deal with life on their own?

Perhaps the answer lay in finding some sort of middle road where I could believe in God, receive eternal life, but just accept that I must run my own show here on Earth. *Was literal interpretation and belief in the infallibility of the scriptures for those who had a more simplistic approach? Supposing all I had been taught about God having a plan and purpose for each individual was erroneous, and I grasped after something that didn't exist?* I had prayed and believed and exercised faith, and God had not answered my prayers. *Maybe it was time to throw in the towel and face the fact I had been mistaken in my beliefs.*

The turmoil raged; questions thundered. In between the raging and the thunder, the sweetly reasonable voice of the Deceiver whispered in my ear, urging me to turn aside and take a different path, one that assuredly held many attractions and advantages. In a mental tennis match, I batted the thoughts backwards and forwards—give up or hang on?

Was Christianity real? How did it work in everyday life?

Then, like a pinpoint of light piercing through blackness, the first inkling of self-knowledge emerged, an awareness of a previously unrecognized character trait. My mind wanted to put the pieces together, to understand the big picture. I identified how I wrestled with something until I could come to terms with it. Plodding determination and tenacity were built into the fiber of my being.

My favorite books as a child had been the Hardy Boys and Nancy Drew mysteries. Later I expanded my repertoire to include espionage. I liked nothing better on television than an English "whodunit," a tale set in a sleepy village, where ordinary people do dastardly deeds and a dogged detective unearths and traps the culprit.

I had taken this mindset into my work at Delta Air Lines. Every day I played detective, investigating the customer's tale of woe, requesting reports from staff members, analyzing the information, and then responding clearly and concisely.

Intellectual honesty called for me to take a hard look at my beliefs before I discarded or drastically revised them. On the one hand, church history overflowed with instances of abuse in the name of religion. Current newspaper headlines were a reminder that the abuse continued. Further, it *was* possible I had received erroneous teaching. Sometimes the Deceiver came as an "angel of light," and our view of God became distorted by religious interpretation. Not all error was as easily discernable as the teachings of cult leaders such as Jim Jones and David Koresh or as blatantly questionable as the impassioned messages from some televangelists.

On the other hand, Christianity had thrived for two thousand years. Rulers and governments sanctioned unbelievable cruelty in an effort to stamp it out. Obviously, something very significant and real had made true Christians willing to be burned at the stake for their beliefs. Something sustained them as they faced the bared teeth of lions. What made young men give up everything to take the gospel to primitive Auca Indians in the Amazon jungle of South America only to have their lives ended with a spear through the chest? What made pastors and priests in Eastern Europe endure horrific conditions in prison cells or face a firing squad rather than recant their faith?

I reviewed my life experiences. Despite what seemed like a never-ending personal and spiritual struggle, there were many evidences of God's care. God *had* guided me. He had graciously overruled in the matter of my parents and spared me from a crushing load. His gentle presence and strength had sustained me through dark days and endless nights. I had been prevented from making horrible mistakes by twists of circumstances that were beyond coincidence.

The pieces were not fitting. Was the problem with the pieces or how I tried to fit them together?

Like an ember that encounters a blast of air, something stirred within me. I remembered the words of St. Augustine, "Man's heart strives after unending eternal happiness. Thou hast created us, O Lord, for Thyself, and our heart is restless until it rests in Thee."

Back to the Sinai Desert

My mind transported me back to Mount Sinai, to Moses, the Hebrews, and the invisible God who led them from bondage to freedom. How I yearned to feel free, to breathe deeply and move unhindered by the chains that bound my spirit. I craved rest for my restless heart. Yet, how did I even begin to seek an intimate relationship with God?

I sensed the Exodus story held important clues.

The Hebrews had dwelled in a society ruled by religion and religious practices. The influence of Egyptian gods penetrated and permeated every aspect of life from birth to death—with its anticipated immortality. Their gods were visible, constant reminders of the prominent place they held in the minds and hearts of the people.

I wondered why God chose to uproot the Hebrews and their possessions from Egypt and lead them into the barren wilderness. Surely he could have softened the hearts of Pharaoh and the Egyptian leaders to make life more tolerable, even pleasant for the foreigners. They had lived for centuries in relative peace and comfort. Obviously there was a significant purpose in removing them from Egypt. What was it? The story gripped my heart and mind.

The sight of an acacia bush in the desert, burning yet not consumed, had arrested Moses' attention. By being willing to turn aside and examine this phenomenon, he met Yahweh, God of the Hebrews, for the first time. That encounter changed his life.

There was no visible burning bush before me; no strange phenomenon attracted my attention. But the fire in my mind refused to be quenched. It urged me to turn aside and investigate.

A Huge Gamble

I've always been too cautious—and cheap—to be a gambler. I once blew $5.00 on the slot machines and quit. I don't like uncertainty, taking chances, and facing the risk of failure, much preferring to see the path before me clearly laid out with illuminated markers along the way. Yet, I now felt inexorably drawn toward the biggest gamble of my life.

"Supposing you spend time and effort checking it out, only to discover in the end that Christianity, belief in one true God, doesn't work as claimed? That life is hard, and then you die?" the Deceiver whispered. "You'll have gambled and lost."

"True," my heart responded. "It *is* a gamble, and I may lose. But what if I win? What if I find a faith worth dying for, one that makes life worthwhile?"

"This could take a lifetime! Think what you might miss along the way?"

"Also true. I might say with my last breath, 'It was all a myth.' But at least I will have checked it out *for myself.*"

The mental conversation bounced back and forth, as the voice of the Deceiver pointed out the potential costs of my decision. My quest for a living faith called for abandonment in pursuit of something intangible related to an invisible God. It bore no resemblance to the sure thing I wanted out of life. It asked me to set aside my plans while I investigated questions that could provide unwanted answers. But the God of the burning bush kept the flame in my mind alive, urging me to take a leap into exploring the unknown.

My father quoted many scriptures in my growing-up years. One of my least favorite was "But seek ye first the kingdom of God, and his righteousness; and all these things shall be added unto you."[6] This was definitely not my preferred order! I wanted the "all things" first. But following my course had left me a sad-eyed, unhappy person who bumped along on the road of life. Maybe it was time to seek God first?

It was a daunting prospect. I questioned how, or if, I could sort through the confusion of differing religious interpretations and find Truth—if indeed it *could* be found. I would have to wipe the slate of my mind clean and start from scratch examining my beliefs about God and His ways, beliefs formed by my grandparents over a century ago and instilled in me from the day I opened my eyes.

Without conscious realization, I embarked on a parallel journey with the Hebrews. To my dismay, the path led directly into the desert, and I found myself alone, all distractions removed, with only a hint of the presence of an invisible God.

POINTER: Review the Origins of Your Concept of God

- Have you ever considered the sources of your ideas about God?

- Did they come from parents and family members?

- Sunday School teachers? School? Television or radio preachers? Church? Professing Christians?

- Books? Magazines? Movies?

- List what you think are God's character traits.

- How accurate do you think your concept of God is?

POINTER REFLECTIONS:

PART TWO

SHAKY PROPS

4

THE FAITH OF MY FATHER(S)

We all come from the past, and children ought to know what it was that went into their making, to know that life is a braided cord of humanity stretching up from time long gone, and that it cannot be defined by the span of a single journey from diaper to shroud.

—Russell Baker

The sun streamed through the windows of the small meeting hall in Johannesburg, South Africa, that afternoon in 1908. Family members and friends filled the rough benches, while at the altar a clergyman posed the traditional question:

"Do you, Archibald Haigh Cooper, take this woman, Constance Henrietta Schumann, to be your lawful wedded wife . . . ?"

The twenty-five-year-old English businessman turned to his twenty-one-year-old Dutch/German bride and responded, "I do."

On that September day, the first pieces of my framework were put in place. Religious, political, and personal threads, once disparate, would unite and blend to create the strands of the tapestry of my life.

Few families have the luxury of well-documented texts, especially those at the turn of the twentieth century in a young country with haphazard record-keeping. Even in later years, when someone documents the highlights in a family's history, the facts are clouded by hazy memory or embellished to enhance the impact of the story.

Fortunately, my grandmother had a literary bent. In 1930 she put together an 80-page diary. The preface stated she compiled the information primarily for the benefit of her children "to remind them constantly of God's unfailing care and provision since their birth, and also, to encourage them to continue steadfastly in the truth and the faith of their parents." She could not have imagined the significant part it would play in the life of her eldest grandchild.

The Beginning

My roots plunged deep into the soil of Africa. The first stem of the family tree, Johan Hendrik Lodewyk Schumann II, arrived from Amsterdam, Holland, in 1856. Apparently a strong missionary calling motivated him to venture forth on the hazardous sea journey to the young, untamed settlement at the tip of the continent, initially known as the Cape Colony, later to become the country of South Africa. Although a qualified chemist, within a short while he and his wife devoted their energies to working among the Colored (mixed race) people, teaching English, Dutch, geography, writing, reading, and arithmetic, as well as giving religious instruction.

Johan III was born in 1862, and twenty years later married Maria Helm. The influence of his parents, coupled with his fine mind, steered him toward a career in teaching, with a special emphasis in religion. In 1896 Johan accepted a temporary position with the Post Office in Johannesburg, a booming city about a thousand miles northeast, with its one hundred horseless carriages, a six-story building, and the frenetic pace of a gold-mining center—at least when compared to the rest of Africa.

When the Boer War, the conflict between the British and the Dutch/German citizen farmers, broke out three years later, Johan joined a Boer commando. They were all captured by the British ten days after the commencement of hostilities, and Johan spent nineteen months as a prisoner on the island of St. Helena off the African coast.

The war ended in 1902, and he resumed his teaching career. He enjoyed a position of prominence as a composer, musician, and lecturer, as well as editor of *De Transvaaler-Zuidafrika*, one of the first newspapers in the area. Johan and Maria produced seven children, five girls and two boys. Their middle daughter Constance, "Connie," would become my grandmother.

Just prior to the end of the Boer War, nineteen-year-old Archibald Cooper left his mother and sisters in Liverpool, England, and boarded a ship headed for the Cape Colony to seek his fortune. Caught in the conflict, Archie signed up with the South African Constabulary, which supported the British troops. The senseless slaughter of battle, coupled with his own wounds, sickened him, leaving an unshakeable emptiness inside.

One evening, he wandered into a tent service conducted by Gypsy Smith, an English evangelist. Although he made an intellectual decision to follow Christ, Archie struggled against relinquishing a self-indulgent lifestyle for what he viewed as the narrow path of a Christian. It took two more years of searching and questioning before he came to the point of making a full commitment. This was followed by a burning desire to find a seminary and study for the ministry.

When Archie's importing firm in Cape Town closed, he accepted a position in Johannesburg. One day he came across a flyer advertising meetings conducted by two American missionaries, John G. Lake and Tom Hezmalhalch, in a small hall. The startling claims in the flyer caught his attention—demonstrations of miracles of healing and other supernatural signs. Archie decided to investigate. It was a pivotal decision.

Caught Up in the Tide of Revivalism

The events taking place were the consequence of the tide of religious zeal that had swept the country of Wales at the turn of the century. What started as a small stream in a chapel in the coal-mining town of New Quay gained momentum until it overflowed across Great Britain. Welsh evangelist Evan Roberts played a prominent role in the conversion of more than 100,000 people to Christianity in the space of six months.[7] The spark to this renewed fervor was the belief that the contemporary church could, and should, experience the "glory of the apostolic New Testament church." This meant stunning conversions, miracles of healing, and an encounter with the supernatural power of God as described in the Book of Acts in the Bible (the "Baptism in the Holy Spirit").

In 1904-05, reports of the revival in Wales reached Los Angeles, and people gathered to seek for a similar reawakening in the United States. Frontier revivalism thrived; prayer sessions and altar calls encouraged personal salvation and exhorted holiness. One of the groups formed the kernel of what later became known as the Azusa Street Mission, the parent of the Apostolic Faith Mission organization. A new religious denomination, the Pentecostals, was born.

As the doctrine of the "spiritual gift of languages" (tongues) grew, people who believed they had received this gift began to travel abroad in order to spread the good news of the Gospel. John G. Lake and Tom Hezmalhalch, along with their families, sailed to South Africa and brought with them the teachings and practices of the early Pentecostals and the Azusa Street Mission. They arrived in Johannesburg in May 1908 and immediately began holding services in a poor area of town.

Their radical doctrine attracted many people, including Johan Schumann, to the point where the small hall overflowed. Intrigued by events, Johan opened his large home to accommodate the crowds—every evening for ninety days.

Delightful, dedicated Constance Schumann caught Archie Cooper's attention, and friendship blossomed into romance. The couple shared a conviction that God had not only called them individually into ministry, but as a ministering married couple. Despite their political differences, Johan agreed to the match. Perhaps shared religious beliefs helped Johan and Archie overcome their opposing views.

Following his marriage, Archie continued with his prospering import-export business, and he and Connie remained involved with the mainline denominational church they attended while enthusiastically aligning themselves with the missionaries' teaching. In Connie's words, the missionaries brought them "light and revelation from the scriptures"—an expanded view of what the Christian life could be, asking and expecting supernatural intervention in ordinary circumstances.

Not surprisingly, when they began to introduce this at their church, they ran headlong into conflict with the leadership. Archie was told to stop promoting "that doctrine." So convinced were they of the merits of what they had learned, they interpreted this to mean "choose between God's Word and the church." Connie wrote,

> We know that God has not changed, that Jesus is the same yesterday, today, and forever, and that He said, "though heaven and earth pass away, my Word shall not pass away," then the commission He gave His disciples must be the same too. But this is not accepted in denominational churches, and the man who preaches the "whole counsel" of God must do so outside the church and be prepared for persecution

in this present century, as it was in John Wesley's time in the 18th century.

The early Pentecostals taught that Christians could, and should, expect similar evidences of Jesus' activity in the lives of individuals as he had demonstrated while on Earth. To not accept this meant that churches were merely spreading the "traditions of men." In their minds, Archie and Connie had no choice but to break away from the traditional church and forge a new path of sharing and teaching the "greater truth" they had received.

The notion of "stepping out in faith" and "completely trusting God" became widely accepted in Pentecostal circles around the world. Smith Wigglesworth summed up the collective thinking of this new movement: "Fear looks—faith jumps. Faith never fails to obtain its object. If I leave you as I found you, I am not God's channel. I am not here to entertain you, but to get you to the place where you can laugh at the impossible."[8]

Bedrock Belief: Literal Interpretation of Scripture

Family members proudly related the story of how Archie and Connie ventured forth into the ministry. Archie read that when Jesus sent out his disciples, they took nothing with them, nor did they have sponsors.[9] Jesus had undoubtedly established a pattern for all to follow, so Archie set about liquidating business assets and called in an auctioneer to handle the sale of his home and possessions. He then gave away the total pro-ceeds of the sale to pay the debts of other Christians, as was done in the early Apostolic church.[10]

That first night after the dissolution of the home, Connie asked Archie where he would sleep, to which he replied, "I don't know." Such "faith" drew admiration from all those with whom they associated.

With no means of support other than meager offerings, Connie and Archie lived in abject poverty. The furnishings in their tiny home in their first ministry base in Middleburg consisted of a wobbly table, two chairs, a kerosene stove, two single beds, a packing case for a cupboard, three small boxes nailed together to make a washstand, and a metal trunk in which they kept their few clothes.

Someone gave Archie a bicycle so he could extend his ministering opportunities. Someone else contributed an old safari hat; yet another gave him a black tailcoat. He'd go off on his rounds to preach or to pray for the sick—pedaling furiously down dusty roads, coattails flapping in the breeze, with his white safari hat securely perched on his head.

Connie described the rigors of Archie's pioneering ministry:

> To reach surrounding farms, my husband had to cycle 30, 40, and 50 miles a day. Only those who know that part of the country can appreciate what this meant to him. The hills were very steep, in fact so much so that in places it was impossible to cycle and he was therefore compelled to tramp for miles and miles. When coming home, he would often be so covered with dirt and dust that I could hardly recognize

him. His food on these trips consisted of
dry corn meal and biltong (dried meat).
But the joy of bringing the Full Gospel
to those dear people and seeing God's
power revealed in their souls and bodies
was worth more than all this to him.

Hostility still ran high in the country after the Boer
War, and Archie, an Englishman and former British
supporter, felt the aftermath of this as he preached and
ministered to people who were primarily of Dutch/
German descent. There were language barriers, as well
as political barriers. Further, the country reeled from
the economic effects of the conflict. The population
of Middleburg consisted of poor farmers and itinerant
workers. Those who had money were not in the least
interested in supporting this English preacher with the
odd outfit who preached a radical doctrine. Archie was
attacked and beaten several times.

Nevertheless, the couple's commitment to God and
resolve to do what they believed He had called them to
do was firm. A cause greater than themselves consumed
them.

Bedrock Belief: Look to God to Provide

Those early days' stories conveyed a passion for ministry and a willingness to endure whatever hardships
were necessary to accomplish the goal of preaching the
gospel and praying for the sick and needy. To Archie
and Connie, "living by faith" meant that if they devoted
themselves fully to the Lord's work, He would provide
for their physical necessities. The pioneering spirit of

the settlers became channeled into a pioneering ministry, and zeal overshadowed personal needs.

Soon after her marriage, Connie got pregnant—the first of fourteen times. The baby, Ruth, arrived healthy but died within the year from meningitis. Among all the stories handed down involving supernatural healings, the details of the death of this baby and the reaction of her parents were buried with her. Instances of answered prayer were broadcast; unanswered prayers were shrouded in silence, attributed to the mysteries of "God's will."

The next pregnancy resulted in the arrival of the daughter who would become my mother, Dorothy (Dossie). Thereafter, babies arrived about every two years. Eight children survived to adulthood.

Babies presented new needs, new demands—they could not live on a staple diet of corn meal and beef jerky. What emerged from Connie's writings is the picture of a young woman whose husband communicated the message she should look to God to provide for her needs, not him. Connie related what happened shortly after my mother's birth:

> When Dorothy was twelve days old, my husband came to take us to our little home. And as I was gathering my necessary things, he whispered to me, "You know we have practically nothing in the home and I have no money." While he was telling me this, the lady of the house where I had been staying was somewhere at the back. As we went forward to thank

her for her love and kindness, she called me and handed me a parcel. Upon arriving home, we found that a good deal of the things that we required were in that very parcel.

As needs arose, Connie did what she had been taught to do—she turned to God in prayer.

When Dorothy was about four weeks old, I was still feeling very weak and an intense longing possessed me for a plate of good soup. But I did not mention this to anyone, not even to my husband. There was nothing in the home to use for soup. However, I said to myself, "Well, if the Lord thinks that I really need this nourishment, He is able to supply the need."

Around tea time, a rap came at the back door, and there stood a young person with a bowl of hot soup. The bearer brought a message from the lady who prepared it that she hoped Connie didn't object to her sending the soup—she just thought it would do her good, her baby being so young.

Connie's interpretation of such instances of God's gracious intervention was always positive, an expression of gratitude to a loving Heavenly Father. And God, in His mercy, did wonderfully provide for her. She makes no mention of Archie making any attempt to get work in order to provide for the physical necessities of his family. It was much more important that he preach the gospel.

Reading Grandma Connie's diary gave me the first inkling of how human interpretation influenced—and distorted—scripture. The teachers chose to selectively apply certain verses to support their beliefs. They failed to present the fact that the Apostle Paul supplemented his income in his early days of ministry by using his tent-making skills.

Bedrock Belief: Faith Healing

The missionaries taught good health was the right of every Christian. Archie and Connie purposed that no doctor would attend them or their children, regardless of the circumstances. This conviction bore no relation to Christian Science. They did not deny the reality of matter—or of pain—nor did they say they did not suffer when they did. Basing their belief on the scripture "Jesus Christ is the same yesterday and today and forever,"[11] they determined "Christ Jesus would be our healer, and that we would trust Him for the healing of our children too. To preach Divine healing and not practice or experience that power in our own lives, we agreed, was being inconsistent." Archie's near death from enteric fever, his refusal to seek medical help, and his subsequent restoration to health after prayer made them more resolute. While they did not speak disparagingly about the medical profession to the children, it was their belief that doctors were for those who did not know the God who heals.

Connie and Archie took three of their six children to England by ship. On the return voyage, Gladys, aged two, became seriously ill with a high temperature and indications of inflammation of the lungs. Connie did what she could to treat the illness, but the steward said he could not bring the light meals she requested without getting the ship's doctor involved. The doctor came, confirmed the diagnosis of inflammation of the lungs, and prescribed medicine. Connie told him that none of their children had ever tasted medicine— they trusted God. The doctor responded, "I don't care what you believe in, that child is very ill, and this inflammation must spread before it breaks. I'm sending the medicine." Which he did. And it sat on the shelf while Gladys's condition deteriorated. That evening the doctor came to see her and then said, "She is bad, you must not lift her. We are coming to the worst part of the voyage and this inflammation must spread before it breaks."

After the doctor left the cabin, Connie passed along the physician's advice to Archie. He responded:

> "Connie, we have preached Divine Healing and believed in the Lord to be our healer, and now we are faced with this serious illness in Gladys, and it may be that the Lord will see fit to take her, and that we will have the sorrow of burying her at sea and arriving home without her. Also, I will be brought before the magistrate in Cape Town because we have not given her any medicine. Are you prepared to stand with me?"
>
> "Yes, certainly."
>
> "Where is the medicine?"

She gave him the bottle, and he threw it through the porthole and left the cabin.

In desperation, Connie picked up her Bible, laid her hand on Gladys, and prayed. Almost instantly the child took a turn for the better. To Connie, this healing was a direct result of their resolute faith and obedience to what they believed about God's Word.

Bedrock Belief: Speaking in Tongues

According to the missionaries, "speaking in tongues" was an initial evidence of the "Baptism in the Holy Spirit." This supernatural experience was a requirement in order to enjoy spiritual power and a more intimate connection with God.

Great-grandfather Johan recorded his impression of what transpired in Lake's and Hezmalhalch's meetings:

> They preached what was in those days considered to be a very strange and startling doctrine, and were looked upon by many as peculiar Christians. If they preached a startling doctrine, the results of their preaching were even more startling. They preached the Baptism of the Holy Ghost with initial evidence of "speaking in tongues." Numbers did indeed receive that Baptism and did indeed speak in tongues.

In fact, he told of a specific instance when one of his daughters spoke fluent Chinese—understood by a Chinese missionary working in the gold mines. Such stories caused a tremendous stir in the religious community and sparked the flame of evangelistic fervor.

Bedrock Belief: Education and Structure Are Suspect

The early Pentecostals believed structure stifled the free working of the Spirit of God in services and therefore discouraged formal study. Sermons were typically unscripted. The preachers placed little emphasis on learning to accurately interpret scripture. Congregation members contributed as they felt "led by the Spirit." Archie relied on what the missionaries taught, what other people told him, and his own understanding and interpretation of what he read in the Bible. He cast aside his original plan to attend seminary.

When a rift occurred among the Apostolic Faith Mission leaders, Tom Hezmalhalch left John Lake in South Africa and returned to California. Henry Turney, an Azusa Street evangelist, had joined his colleagues in South Africa in 1909, becoming pastor of a congregation in Pretoria. Dissension caused Turney to break away from the Apostolic Faith Mission. He turned over his congregation in Pretoria to Archie, who formed a new Pentecostal denomination, the Full Gospel Church.

Solidifying Their Beliefs

Undeterred by criticism, Archie clung tenaciously to his beliefs and preached them with the intensity of a zealot. Each new "miracle" of healing or incident that, in his thinking, affirmed his views only made him more single-minded. The freedom from structure promoted by the Pentecostals gave him the "freedom" to choose his areas of emphasis and place his own application on scripture. He focused on the sensational rather than the quiet, powerful inner working of God in an individual's life. Speaking in tongues, prophesying, giving interpretations, miraculous healings, and other visible/audible displays demonstrated and affirmed the Pentecostal experience—and his ministry. The "fruit" of the Spirit—love, joy, peace, patience, kindness, goodness, faithfulness, gentleness, self-control—took second place to the "gifts" of the Spirit. This reliance upon the spectacular formed an integral part of the core beliefs passed along to his children and his children's children—me.

In relating these stories, Connie added a note of caution:

> The reader must not conclude from these incidents and answers to prayer, everything just came at the identical moment that we asked for it. Oh, no! On many occasions our faith was tested and we were kept waiting for the answer. But we never doubted the fact that God heard and was mindful of our need, and that He would never fail us or cause His precious word to lack fulfillment in our lives.

POINTER: Examine Your Core Beliefs

- What were your family background beliefs, e.g., Mainline Protestant, Catholic, Conservative Fundamentalist, Pentecostal (Charismatic), Jewish, New Age, Modern Liberal, Agnostic, or Atheistic?

- Do you know the basis for these beliefs?

- Which ones did you accept?

- Which have you discarded?

POINTER REFLECTIONS:

5

TWO DIFFERENT WORLDS MERGE

In 1924, Archie decided to leave Pretoria and move his wife and six children to the city of Durban on the southeastern coast. Once more, he attributed this to God's leading. I'm glad he did move, as this lovely resort city would eventually be my birthplace.

Nothing awaited Archie in Durban, no home, no sponsorship, simply a small tin shack where a handful of people gathered each Sunday. He had little hope of financial support as his family outnumbered the congregation. Despite his earnest endeavors, there were no new converts added to the church during the next two years. He considered packing up and moving to Australia, hoping for better success in his ministry efforts. Then, in 1926, a member of a large family wandered into a service. Soon they all began attending, and the ranks of membership swelled. Talk of moving to Australia ceased.

To help cover the expenses of his large family, Archie took in paying boarders—not missionary recruits as he had done in Pretoria. He pulled eleven-year-old Dossie out of school to help in the home. Then Archie expanded her role.

Connie played the piano a little and taught her eldest daughter the basics. No sooner had she learned a few notes than Archie announced she could play for the church services.

"But Daddy, I only know one hymn!" she protested.

"That's all right," he said. "We'll sing that hymn until you learn a new one."

Mom told how being thrust into this position at the young age of fourteen terrified her. Not only did she feel inadequate, but this responsibility meant she had to attend church night after night as her father struggled valiantly to build his congregation. Tiredness overcame her one evening, and resting her head on top of the piano, she fell sound asleep. She roused, startled, when Archie loudly and repeatedly announced the closing hymn.

Thus began Mom's lifetime involvement in church music. She discovered an emotional discharge valve, a means of expressing her inner self. For the rest of her life, people said she had "soul" in her playing.

From Tent to Church Building

By now the Pentecostal influence around the world had taken root and flourished. Traveling missionaries and evangelists added South Africa to their itineraries, and Durban being the main seaport to the interior, they visited with Archie and Connie. The congregation had outgrown the little green church, so Archie purchased a tent and erected this on a piece of vacant land. Stephen and George Jeffreys had been added to the growing ranks of English Pentecostal evangelists, and Stephen, in particular, drew large crowds to his meetings where he preached and prayed for the sick. In 1929 Stephen sailed to South Africa. "In Durban a great tent was packed to capacity and God moved in such power that a beautiful church was subsequently erected on the site with a great congregation filling it."[12]

It was the turning point in Archie's church.

The impetus of those tent meetings inspired Archie to build a permanent structure for his congregation. The story of its construction became a highlight in the historical records of the Full Gospel Church.

The local church council secured a plot of land with the goal of building, but the financial depression sweeping the world hit the South African economy. Almost all construction ceased. No bank, building society, or individual would lend Archie money. Undeterred, he purposed to act in faith and take on the responsibility himself. It was a day-by-day venture, scrounging materials from builders who had no business themselves, paying workmen as funds became available, and motivating the congregation to pray and give. In June 1932, he dedicated the building to the Glory of God, and the circumstances surrounding its construction became a much-repeated tribute to Archie's faith in overcoming adversity.

Closed Door, Open Door

I loved the story of how a twist of circumstances sent Dossie to England. William F. P. Burton, founder of the Congo Evangelistic Mission, regularly visited South Africa to recruit missionaries. Inspired by tales of his efforts to teach and minister to the Congolese people, Dossie decided this was her vocation. She sensed a pull into some sphere of ministry, but the thought of taking any type of leadership role frightened her. Going to work in the Congo seemed ideal—nobody would question her ability, and she could faithfully serve God while remaining anonymous. Her application, however, was rejected. Malaria, blackwater fever, and other diseases of the region took such a toll on the missionaries that only those candidates in top physical condition were accepted. A succession of illnesses had weakened Dossie, making her ineligible. She was devastated.

Archie and Connie dreamed that their children would follow in their footsteps and go into ministry. Claude, at seventeen, showed promising signs. When the door of missionary activity in the Congo closed to Dossie, they suggested she go to England to study at Elim Bible College for a year. Somehow they found the money to pay for her one-way fare, if nothing else. At age nineteen, she boarded a ship on her own, headed for Southampton. Her life would never be the same.

Englishman Jack

The man who would one day become my father arrived on the scene in Romford, Essex, on the East Side of London, England, in 1905. Christened John Frederick Wooderson, true to English culture, he went by "Jack." The family consisted of father Walter, a railway policeman, mother Alice, and older brother by two years, Walter, Jr.

A sensitive child with a quiet, serious nature, Jack won a medal from the Boy Scouts for heroism in rescuing a drowning child, an early indication of his selfless disposition. He and his mother attended the local Church of England parish where he served as an acolyte and choirboy.

At sixteen Jack contracted tuberculosis. He grew so weak and sickly he could no longer attend school, and his mother devoted herself to nursing her son through what she believed would be his final months.

Word got around town one day about Evangelist Stephen Jeffreys' meetings. Stories of astounding healings made Alice determined to get her son to a service. Neighbors helped with transportation. Mr. Jeffreys prayed for Jack—and Alice's prayers were answered. Her boy gained strength and was soon well enough to finish school, after which he started an apprenticeship as a wireless mechanic. No doctor who saw him thereafter could find a trace of scars on his lungs from TB.

But something more than healing took place on that occasion. Jack said God called him into the ministry. His mother supported his decision. His father disowned him.

He enrolled at Elim Bible College in Clapham, London, as a day student. At night he returned to his sparsely furnished rented attic room. He told how he gazed longingly at the warm fire in the landlady's parlor as he passed on his way up the stairs. There he wrapped himself in a blanket, ate his cold meal, and prepared to study the Bible. Despite hardship, cold, hunger, and mistreatment, his commitment to God and the ministry never wavered. He was still attending the College as a ministry intern when he met lively, boisterous Dossie, newly arrived from South Africa.

Strolling by the piano in the dining area, Dossie picked up a hymnbook. Written on the flyleaf was the name "John F. Wooderson." Curious, she asked a friend about the book's owner and was instantly regaled with descriptions of the handsome, tall, black-haired, blue-eyed young minister who bore the name.

Some subtle maneuvering on the part of a few friends threw them together on a car ride. Amazingly, this reserved, English clergyman plucked up the courage to ask the young lady to have afternoon tea with him. It was not love at first sight. Mom told how they were complete opposites in temperament and came from different worlds. But they shared a love for God and a commitment to ministry. The friendship grew, and before the year ended, Jack proposed marriage, Dossie accepted, and they became engaged. A major obstacle stood in their way—her imminent return home. Saying goodbye at the docks at Southampton, neither of them had any idea when, or even if, they would meet again. They prayed together and agreed to leave the matter in God's hands.

The voyage back to Durban took almost three weeks. As soon as the crane connected the gangplank to the ship so guests could board, Grandpa Archie hurried to find Mom. With the air of someone heralding tremendous news, he announced, "Dorothy, your young man is coming out to South Africa on the next ship to be my assistant."

I'm not sure Mom gave her "young man" an accurate picture of her large, exuberant family. They were noisy, lively, and outgoing; Jack was painfully shy. He said he spent his days dealing with constant flushes of embarrassment while his fiancée's siblings mocked his bright red face. Further, the sun and heat of South Africa made this very prim and proper Englishman uncomfortable. It took Dad years to gather the courage to wear shorts in the blazing summer.

Their road to true love was not smooth. The differences in temperament that whispered in England shrieked in South Africa. Mom called off the engagement and gave back the ring. Dad, in typical manner, graciously accepted it—until Mom became aware of the long line of young ladies ready to step into her place. She recanted, and Grandpa Archie performed the marriage ceremony on December 2, 1932.

The woman Dad married had a lively intelligence, a sense of humor that entertained everyone around her, and a deep love for God and music. Uneducated, she had a lawyer's mind and could argue her way out of any situation. Untrained, she had a flair for drama. She would have loved being on the stage. I could imagine her in some repertory company as, chameleon-like, she became absorbed in portraying her character, or with script in hand, directed the whole show. But in those days and in her environment, the stage was considered a "worldly" profession. So she chose to marry Jack.

From her side, Mom married a gentleman, and a gentle man, a man of conviction, courage, and unblemished character. Gracious, self-sacrificing, an optimist who looked for the best in everything and everyone. Never a go-getter except in the realm of "exercising faith," he acceded to Mom's wishes—and demands— in almost everything. He rarely talked about his home or family, and years later I would understand why. But Dossie and Jack made a "'til death do us part" commitment to each other and to ministry.

Both were Pentecostal by belief and experience and, for the most part, upheld what Grandpa Archie and Grandma Connie believed—faith healing, miracles, and speaking in tongues. Years later I would realize how Dad's Anglican upbringing—and English reserve— tempered his Pentecostal practices.

A Shattering Blow

Three years into the marriage, Dossie got pregnant. Anticipation ran high in the family at the prospect of the arrival of the first grandchild, and great-grandchild.

Mom and Dad never told me the details of what happened that fateful year. Mom vaguely referred to what she termed an "inquisition" conducted by the church leaders. By now the Pentecostal movement had gained strength, and the small, scattered churches were formed into an organization. She told how she sat for days, listening as the church leadership grilled her father and husband about alleged problems. I concluded from her comments that the difficulty was related to the church and its membership. Telling me the unvarnished truth, although painful, would have spared me years of misdirected simmering hostility.

Mom shared how anger welled up within her. She wanted nothing more to do with direct involvement in ministry. Disillusioned, hurt, she made the decision to devote her energies exclusively to her husband and unborn child. Jack could look after the church; she would look after him and the baby.

The day came when Dossie was rushed to the hospital for the birth of her child. After an excruciatingly painful and slow labor, she delivered a beautiful baby girl—still born. The infant strangled in the umbilical cord. Jack was heartbroken. Dossie was devastated. The whole family, plus church members, mourned the loss and questioned how God could allow this to happen to Pastor and Mrs. Wooderson. It simply wasn't fair. They were dealing with the age-old question of why bad things happen to good people.

Jack would later credit this experience with teaching him empathy for those in his "flock" who mourned. He said that previously he had ministered out of head knowledge, now he could minister from the heart out of his deeply personal grief.

Dossie's interpretation was that God had taken her child as punishment for her rebellion against the ministry. Contrite and broken, she made a renewed commitment to put God and service to Him first in her life. It was a decision that resulted in untold good for the benefit of others, and untold harm to her daughters.

POINTER: Family Decisions and Attitudes Shape Who We Become

- What major decisions of your parents or grandparents influenced the person you are today, e.g., relocation, career change, education?

- Do you consider these positive, negative, or neutral?

- If negative, is there anything you can do to change the effects?

- Can you learn to accept the outcome?

POINTER REFLECTIONS:

6
FORMING IDEAS ABOUT GOD

Train up a child in the way he should go: and when he is old, he will not depart from it.

Proverbs 22:6 (KJV)

My parents told me I was born at Mother's Hospital in Durban. However, all my life I suspected this was not the truth. I believe I was born in my dad's church, that the order of service briefly halted as my mother slipped away, delivered me, and then went back to playing the piano for the congregation. I'm convinced I took my first breath in church.

Mom and Dad's sadness after the loss of their first child turned to jubilation when I arrived, healthy and starving. I came into the world with a love of food, something which never diminished.

My appearance caused a momentary pause in the tempo of ministry, but soon Dad, Mom, and baby were off to church together. Three years later, my sister Claudia expanded the family and added another member to the congregation.

Like most preachers' kids and those born into Christian homes, an awareness of God began to envelop me somewhere between the time of opening my little eyes and taking my first steps. Mom and Dad said prayers over me, and subconsciously I absorbed the idea there was someone who listened to what they said. Sitting in a highchair, I was taught to fold my hands and close my eyes during grace at mealtimes. I grew up in an environment where God was recognized, respected, even feared. Similar to parents playing classical music to a baby in the womb, I began absorbing the convictions of my parents, grandparents, and family members.

Before many years passed, I realized my religious exposure surpassed that of my peers. I discovered I had been born into a unique and prominent family. My grandparents pioneered the Pentecostal denomination in South Africa and had founded the church I attended every Sunday. The stories of their exploits in the realm of "exercising faith" to bring about God's miraculous intervention connected with my growing sense of adventure. My eyes widened as family members related details of their zeal to preach the gospel and spread their beliefs, regardless of personal cost.

I soon picked up on the message that church was the absorbing interest in our home, the pivot around which everything else swirled. The pace of life ebbed and flowed depending on where we were in relation to Sunday.

On no day of the week did our home more resemble a well-oiled machine than on Sundays. The energy level accelerated. Mom's organizational skills kicked into high gear. Switching to her inspector role, she made sure her girls were clean, dressed in their best clothes, and ready to be presented to the Lord and the congregation. Then she turned her attention to herself. We used to kid her that she soaped the bath and merely slid in one end and out the other on Sundays. Finally, we assembled in the car and headed down the road to participate in the most important event of the week. Dad wore a white "dog-collar," black jacket, and striped black and white pants. On arriving at church, I found Grandpa Archie wore a similar outfit. This, apparently, was how preachers dressed.

My family believed children could and should be taught to attend church—and to behave while there. The idea of a nursery or playroom was still in the incubation stage in our early years. Claudia and I each had a small pillow and blanket, and with these tucked under our arms, we paraded down to the front pew next to the piano Mom played. We had books and crayons to quietly amuse ourselves. Eventually we grew to the point where we became interested in observing and participating in the first part of the service. But Dad's announcement of the sermon topic signaled the time to spread our blankets and pillows and settle down to sleep. It's a good thing my father didn't depend upon his daughters for support and encouragement during his sermons.

How well I remember hanging around for what seemed like an eternity each week, waiting for Dad to finish shaking hands with his "flock" or for him to appear after a prayer session with someone in need. Finally, he'd give us the nod to head for the car. Wearily, Claudia and I settled into each corner of the back seat to snooze our way home. Another Sunday was over. Ahead of us lay Monday and school.

Sundays truly were Us!

Learning About God

Every morning, from as far back as I can remember, Dad gathered the family for devotions. He or Mom read from *Hurlburt's Stories of the Bible*, we sang a song, then one of them prayed for each member of the family, asking God for protection and help as we faced the day. In the evening we knelt at our beds and said our prayers before settling down to sleep.

The daily and weekly Bible stories taught me the essentials of behavior pleasing, or displeasing, to God, as a colorful array of Old Testament characters presented practical examples of wise and unwise choices. I soaked in the stories, and my fertile imagination embellished each account. I learned about Joseph's steadfast reliance on God in the face of inexplicable circumstances. Esther demonstrated courage by her willingness to put her life on the line to save her people. Abraham exemplified trust as he followed an invisible God who gave extraordinary instructions. I learned about Noah's diligence in obeying God despite mocking neighbors, and Daniel's unflinching integrity. The way Jesus accepted and respected people was the desired standard of behavior, especially in my multi-cultural environment. Such values became the fabric of my life.

I also heard about Achan's thievery and Sapphira's deceit and its consequences—although lying never presented a problem to me. The God who sees everything undoubtedly had a hotline to my mother and instantly communicated any infraction. To this day, I can only lie when it's of no consequence—as for a surprise party.

These stories gave clear-cut examples of the rewards of obedience versus the penalties of disobedience. I determined not to be on the receiving end of God's displeasure. Without conscious awareness, obedience to God and obedience to Mom began to run together in my mind, like merging rivulets. Since Mom used scripture and Christian example as a means of discipline, disobeying Mom became synonymous with disobeying God.

God and church became as integral components of my environment as the air I breathed and the food I enjoyed. An eager, inquiring mind, coupled with a sensitive nature, made me acutely attuned to my surroundings. I tried hard to grasp the meaning of the instruction I received and worked at deciphering the behavioral clues.

Piece by piece the framework of my understanding about God took form. How did it become such an odd shape? I believe it started with the play.

Prop #1 – A God Who Rescues

Mom released her pent-up dramatic talents once a year on a couple of hundred unsuspecting Sunday school children at the Anniversary program. So powerful were the dramas that it was during one of these I made the decision to accept Jesus as my Savior. I knew all about Jesus, His life, and His death on the cross but made no move to take the step of acting on this knowledge, content to merely enjoy the stories. I had little spiritual inclination—until the night of the play.

The drama depicted Jesus' parable of the ten girls as recorded in Matthew 25. All ten young women took their lamps and settled down to await the arrival of the bridegroom. He delayed, and they became sleepy. Finally, a cry rang out heralding his approach. The hearts of five of the girls plummeted when they realized they had failed to bring along extra oil. The other five had none to spare, so they ran off to buy some. In their absence, the bridegroom came. The women who had wisely made adequate provision for their lamps joyfully went with the bridegroom into the wedding feast, and the door closed. When the remaining five returned, they were denied entrance into the wedding hall. They were too late.

To an impressionable eight-year-old sitting wide-eyed on the front pew, the wailing and weeping of the foolish women was terrifying. When Dad explained at the end of the service that by accepting Jesus as my Savior I could ensure I would not be among those left behind, I immediately stepped forward.

I had no inkling of the love of God or how this connected to the wise young women making adequate preparation for the arrival of the bridegroom. My only frame of reference was the dire consequences of not doing what was right.

Prop #2 – A God of Expectations

No magical transformation occurred that evening. My parents, however, held a different view. Thrilled with my decision, they believed I had made a genuine commitment to Christ. The next step was to begin to exhibit "Christian" conduct.

Mom and Dad's guiding scripture, the focus of their parenting goal, was the verse in Proverbs 22:6: "Train up a child in the way he should go: and when he is old, he will not depart from it." They interpreted this to mean they were to form their children in the way they believed was right according to their understanding of what God wanted and expected. Parenting became a challenge to produce model Christian children who would be visible examples of the model Christian clergy family. Mom earnestly pointed out attitudes or behaviors that did not correspond to "a Christian."

So I learned to be good. Through careful attention and diligent effort, I figured out acceptable behavior. Pleasing God and my parents and retaining their joint favor became crucial.

Prop #3 – A God Who Provides

I was exposed early in life to the practice of presenting needs to God in prayer. All those stories told by my grandparents and parents about amazing intervention from a responsive God had become an integral part of my inherited belief system.

We moved from our cramped apartment into a new home when I was eleven. Dad had managed to secure land earmarked for war veterans. Although exempted from service in World War II, the Ministry of Defense recognized the important role he played in serving the troops who passed through the port of Durban. Dad arranged financing, and a member of the church handled the construction of a double-story brick home with a red-tiled roof on a third of an acre lot. To me, it was a huge mansion.

Preachers in South Africa were generally impoverished in my growing-up days. Most people adopted the attitude, "We'll give him the minimum salary, and God can provide the rest." We were no exception. Candy was a luxury which only came as a result of strongly-encouraged pastoral visits by Dad to a kindly member of the congregation who managed a candy store. Sodas were a Christmas treat.

Claudia and I wanted a carpet for the bare floor in our bedroom, but Dad explained he had no money for this. He suggested we ask God to give us a carpet, and that we specify the color. So, before crawling into bed each evening, we knelt and prayed for a green carpet.

Within a few weeks, Dad received a call from a lady to whom he had ministered.

"I hope you won't be offended, Pastor Wooderson," she stated apologetically, "but I have a green Axminster carpet available, and I wondered if you could use this in your new home."

We were ecstatic—and astounded. God really did answer our prayer. I had no clue how this worked, but I was all in favor of the idea.

Regrettably, this aspect of God became entangled with my natural inclination to drift off into the dream world of *Grimm's Fairy Tales*. My imagination soared into a romantic realm where good always overcame evil, the prince inevitably arrived in the nick of time to rescue the maiden, and all lived happily ever after.

What evolved was an image of a God who was part genie and part fairy godmother, with the generosity of Santa Claus. With a God who could perform the miraculous on my side, the possibilities of having all my wishes come true seemed limitless.

Prop #4 – A God Who Sees and Hears

Mom told us God saw everything, everywhere. Not only did he see everything, he heard everything. While I could not fathom the concept of an invisible God who watches, I knew Santa Claus was real—I'd seen him in the department store. If somehow Santa could keep up with my behavior, then I guessed God could, too. I wanted the best from both, so I made a supreme effort to mind my p's and q's.

I was not a willful child—at least not overtly. I simply wanted acceptance, attention, and love. Mom spoke admiringly of my teachable attitude and how I listened attentively. She had the innate skill of a trial lawyer in presenting her arguments. Coupled with scripture references, who was I to argue? I would invariably "see the light" and obey.

But I grew wary. The world outside, which had previously beckoned with adventure, revealed a fearful side. It wasn't safe to make mistakes. I needed to learn how to do it right—whatever "right" might be.

Long after Santa Claus faded from reality, the idea of a God who watched remained. Instead of creating a comforting awareness of His care, Mom's worthy motives contributed to my forming the view of God as "Heavenly Policeman." This distortion quickened the pace of the performance treadmill and kept me panting most of my life.

Prop #5 – A God Who Helps

School was an inconvenient encroachment on playtime and something to be endured between vacation periods. My good memory enabled me to skim along with minimal effort for several years. However, exams generated sweaty palms and rising panic, mainly over the fact that if I didn't pass I would have to do the year over, which was unthinkable.

Mom and Dad encouraged us to ask God for help at these times, and in family devotions Dad earnestly added his prayers. I don't believe Claudia or I ever faced a major test, academic or music, that hadn't been prayed over beforehand. While this dependence on God to refresh my memory played into my tendency to coast, it did establish a lifelong habit of asking God for help in times of need.

Prop #6 – A God Who Heals

"Joy, stand up straight. You're slouching again." These words became so familiar I hardly heard them.

I don't remember what prompted my mother to take me to a doctor to investigate this tendency, but it must have been regressing. I heard the words "scoliosis" and "back brace" as my parents reviewed the medical diagnosis. Next thing, I was exempted from gym at high school—no great loss as the pummel horse and I never did become friends.

At that time, Mom was one of the few organists in the country. I heard talk that Oral Roberts would be coming to South Africa to hold faith healing services, and Mom had been asked to play. Since both my parents believed fervently in faith healing, they decided to take me with them on the 400-mile drive to Johannesburg to have Mr. Roberts pray over me.

I entered the vast tent and seated myself on a fold-up chair on the end of a row. Mom sat at the organ and Dad on the platform as one of the ministerial dignitaries. When the call for prayer came, I moved forward as instructed, somewhat apprehensive over the noise and charged emotions around me. Oral Roberts put a drop of oil on my head, prayed that God would heal my spine, and I returned to my seat. A reporter asked if I had experienced any supernatural touch, to which I replied, "No." It was all rather mystifying. My parents encouraged me to "exercise faith" that I had been healed and dropped all talk about a back brace. I resumed normal activities, concentrating on building strength in my back muscles.

X-rays taken many years later showed signs of arrested scoliosis.

Prop #7 – A God of Obligations

The population of South Africa comprised four major ethnic groups: Whites (English and Afrikaners), Africans (from many indigenous tribes), Indians (those who originally came over from India to work in the sugar cane fields and stayed), and Coloreds (mixed blood descendants of the early settlers).

The city of Durban during my growing-up years comprised approximately 200,000 Whites, 200,000 Africans, and 200,000 Indians. The government mandated that each ethnic group live separately. Dad's church had a large White congregation. He also supervised the African branch and worked closely with the overseer of the Indian members. As a result, everybody knew Pastor Wooderson—or so it seemed. If I stepped out of line, the grapevine would certainly relay the details to Mom and Dad.

Around age seventeen, my longing for independence got the better of me, and I yielded to the temptation of a matinee movie in a theater downtown. The film was *A Night To Remember,* the original story of the sinking of the *S.S. Titanic.* Stifling rising guilt, I took off from the house to meet a friend without telling anyone my intent. With a pounding heart, I sank low in my seat in the theater, fearful of being recognized, while illicit pleasure added to the powerful drama on screen. To my relief, all was calm at home, and it appeared nobody had noticed my absence.

The storm broke a couple of days later. Word of my transgression reached my Aunt Norma, Mom's sister and Dad's associate pastor, who lived with us. She felt it her duty to point out the error of my ways. What kind of Christian example was I, a Sunday school teacher and leader in the youth group? I might have been the cause of someone turning away from God. On and on it went. I listened quietly to the tirade, and when it was over, thought that was the end of the matter. Then another aunt decided to add her condemnation. She told me I had an obligation to my parents not to do anything that would cause embarrassment or bring dishonor to God, the church, and the family. I found it interesting neither Mom nor Dad said a word about my "straying." Possibly they were unaware of what I had done, or they chose to leave the reprimand to my aunts.

Life became a delicate tightrope as I tried to balance everyone's expectations. I learned my role and played it almost to perfection. My emerging identity became submersed in the larger identity of being "Pastor Wooderson's daughter." Someone later told me, "Joy, knowing your parents, I imagine people must have expected you to be a spiritual giant by the age of twelve!"

Prop #8 – A Distant God

Our fathers invariably form the basis on which our early conception of God is founded. Dad was kind, gentle, and good. His equable temperament and reserved English demeanor gave him an air of quiet dignity. Add to this his devotion to God and commitment to Christian behavior and he became quite saintly. My own, and others' impression of Dad was crystallized in an incident that occurred many years later.

A five-year-old went to "big" church for the first time. Michael was quite attentive, wriggling to the edge of the pew to watch the brilliant pianist. Shoulder-length locks flowed around his ears as his body moved with each run of his fingers over the keyboard. Then Dad stepped up to the pulpit to read the scripture. Thick, silvery hair capped an unlined face. In his precise English accent, he spoke the words from the King James Version of the Bible. After that, Michael lost interest. During lunch, the boy's grandmother asked him how he enjoyed the worship service.

"Oh, it was great," he replied. "Jesus played the piano, and God read the Bible."

No wonder I based my concept of God on this man. He represented authority, integrity, and a code of behavior. While I admired him enormously, he was emotionally distant. I do not believe this was in any way intentional. He was a product of his era and background. Additionally, his "flock" demanded so much of his time. I accepted this as the price we had to pay for being in a clergyman's family, but the feelings of distance and detachment took root. They were then transferred to my concept of God. God was there; He represented holiness, authority, and standards. But He was a long, long way off from me.

POINTER: Think About Your Childhood Beliefs

- What did you believe about God as a child?

- Did you subscribe to my "Santa Claus/Genie" view, or did God seem terrifying?

- Which view still holds?

- Have you ever examined your concept of God with your critical, adult mind?

POINTER REFLECTIONS:

7

SHOULDS AND OUGHTS

One day I realized Mom and Dad were noticeably happy about something. Claudia had asked to be baptized in the Sunday evening service—a highly visible event. Her request created a predicament. I couldn't let my younger sister outshine me. To not follow her lead would automatically flash to Mom and Dad I had an inferior level of spirituality. So I announced that I, too, wanted to get baptized.

Our church believed in baptism by immersion in water. Because we didn't have a fancy baptismal tank, this part of the service turned into quite a production. While the congregation sang a hymn, several deacons rolled up the carpet, moved the pulpit aside, and lifted and stacked the floorboards to reveal the already filled tank. We often gleefully reminisced about the time one of the deacons missed his footing and fell into the pool.

Once everything was ready, Dad appeared in white shirt and trousers, followed by the female candidates in white dresses, and then the males. After Dad immersed the candidates, they climbed the steps out of the tank to be discreetly wrapped in large towels before they sloshed their way to the change rooms.

Claudia and I donned white outfits, the whole family gathered for the joyous occasion, and Dad immersed both his daughters on the same evening. But by publicly signifying my belief in Christ and water baptism, I unwittingly raised the bar of performance expectations. This was my second major act in response to the "shoulds" and "oughts" being subtly communicated.

What Mom and Dad did not realize, and what I did not understand myself, was my lack of spiritual motivation. In my mind, I had avoided the horrors of being "left behind," yet I sensed growing pressure to conform, like an unseen hand pushing and squeezing me into a desired shape. To admit my confusion might disappoint my parents. In some vague way, I felt this could affect their acceptance of me. I internalized the message that good behavior equated to retaining love, and fear of stepping out of line and incurring my parents' displeasure took root in my mind. Sadly, God and my parents became inextricably intertwined.

The pressure to be the perfect pastor's daughter weighed heavily at church, where many eyes watched my every move. Mom drilled Claudia and me in correct behavior—quietness, sitting still, no running, and above all, no disturbances.

Behavioral Expectations

I knew our church held high standards regarding dress and conduct. Mom and Dad followed the guidelines established by Grandpa Archie and the Pentecostal church in South Africa. Women should not wear slacks, lipstick, eye shadow, or earrings. Movies were forbidden as they could contaminate one's thinking. Dancing invited temptation. Mom monitored the type of music played in the home, and I recall being reprimanded for singing one of the popular nonsense songs that drifted across the Atlantic Ocean from America.

Then I learned God had standards for sisterly behavior.

Claudia and I were as different as night and day in every respect except looks. I liked stories; Claudia liked music. She was quick, agile, athletic; I floated through every day in a daydream. It tried her patience to the limit when I washed and she dried the dishes. In my imagination, the mound of soapsuds became a magnificent castle, which could be refashioned with a dollop here or there. Claudia stood by, dish towel in hand, waiting for me to get the next dish to her.

We got along quite well in our early years since I was a master manipulator. On one occasion we were playing at hairdressers, with me as the beautician, she the customer. Tiring of my fooling with her hair, she wanted to change the game.

"What would you like to play?" I asked sweetly.

"Mommies and Daddies," she replied.

"Fine. You be the little girl, and I'll be the Mommy. Now, I have to fix your hair before you go off to school."

Things continued this way until Claudia got old enough to see through my manipulative practices. Worse yet, she exhibited a razor-sharp mind and could whip out a response to any argument that left me speechless. It was infuriating. I wanted to yell at her, or at the very least, slam a door, but my parents considered such displays inappropriate. We were the minister's daughters and had to set an example for others. We had to demonstrate to all we were different. In their efforts to guide our conduct, we repeatedly heard "Christian girls don't . . ." or "Christian girls should . . ."

Find God's Blueprint Plan

As my understanding developed, I became aware that my parents considered "finding and doing the will of God" second only to the step of accepting Jesus Christ as personal Savior. I picked up that God had a perfect will and a permissive will for each of us. The latter came about when we went our own way and missed out on the former. This belief only solidified in my thinking the necessity of striving to get in on God's "perfect will," reinforced by numerous stories of people who reaped the horrific consequences of failure to do the "will of God." I formed the picture in my mind of a custom-designed blueprint for my life. I only had to find this plan, follow the formula, and life would unfold beautifully, bringing maximum happiness and fulfillment.

The positive consequence of this thinking was that I carefully prayed about all major decisions. The negative was that I developed an erroneous concept of what God wanted and expected.

Service to the Church = Approval (Godly and Parental)

Through Dad's efforts, the church attracted a large number of young people. He committed himself to mentoring and developing leadership within this group, and over the years several individuals went into the ministry or to the mission field. One of the young men was Michael Wenning, who in 2004 conducted President Ronald Reagan's California funeral service.

We were encouraged to take turns participating in some way in the Friday night youth services. I loved "Disguised Bible Characters," a variation on "What's My Line?" We studied a Bible character and presented a five-minute outline of key events and characteristics without giving a name. At the conclusion, the group tried to figure out the individual's identity. When my turn came, I delighted in coming up with some obscure piece of information that drew a red herring across the path of my listeners' thinking. I can see now how this tapped into the way my mind works. Clues, mysteries, problem solving, and analysis were to become an integral part of my life. At the time, however, I was unaware of anything beyond playing around with Bible stories.

Aunt Norma, Dad's assistant minister, appointed me to head up the Beginner Department of the Sunday school. I use the word "appointed" accurately, because few people were able to say no to Norma. As it turned out, those years of involvement with my twenty-five plus two-to-five-year-olds each week were fun. I led the assembly portion with its share of action songs, Claudia played the accordion, and I then let loose with my own dramatic talents in telling the Bible stories.

My involvement generated plenty of positive reinforcement. Norma was passionate about reaching children and teaching them about Jesus. The success of the Beginner Department reflected on her leadership, therefore I was "A-OK."

When I reached nineteen, the kitchen table discussions revolved around the challenges of holding the young people's interest in the church. Some of them had started to stray into "worldly" activities. They needed a Saturday night Youth Club, a place to congregate in a safe environment. The church council agreed to furnish a Ping-Pong table, board games, and books in a house the church owned, and I was asked to be co-leader with one of the guys. I threw myself into this endeavor and took my responsibilities seriously. I felt as though the spiritual health of the youth department rested on my shoulders.

This expanded leadership role developed my organizational and interpersonal skills. I interacted with church members on the refreshment roster, planned each week's activities, played hostess, selected carefully censored movies to screen, and took care of all the administrative details. It was a great training ground, and I carried the lessons learned into my professional life.

It also made me feel accepted in the family. The harder I worked, the more smoothly the club ran, the better the reputation of the youth group and its reflection on Mom, Dad, Norma, and the church. I made a valuable contribution and was being noticed for my efforts. The seeds of equating personal worth with service to God and the church were planted in my mind.

At the time, I had no idea the profound effect the teaching of the Pentecostal church on the doctrine of eternal security would have on my thinking. Eternal security is the belief that once a person truly accepts Jesus Christ as personal Savior and receives forgiveness from sin, that person is forever secure in God's love. Even if he sins and dies before he is again restored to God, his heavenly reward may be diminished, but he does not lose his salvation. God constantly works in the hearts of His children to bring about reconciliation.

Mom told me that when she was in Bible College she did a study on this subject and found that there were almost an equal number of scriptures to support totally opposing views. She concluded she would rather err on the side of being sure than risk the consequences of presumption. It was a case of "better safe than sorry."

What emerged in my mind bordered on performance-based Christianity. God's grace made salvation possible, but after that we had to work at maintaining it. This teaching added a further element of uncertainty and insecurity into my already shaky world. Doing what was expected assumed even greater importance. It also provided ammunition for others to fire at those who had a tendency to "stray," as happened in the incident of my aunt and the movie.

The speed of the performance treadmill picked up, and I ran harder.

A Tangled Skein

By the time I left my teens, my ideas about God were firmly entrenched. I thought I understood all the essential elements of His character and what He required. I trusted my parents and believed implicitly that what they taught me was sound. To do otherwise would have been disloyal.

But I had unwittingly fallen into the trap of building my concept of God on what I wanted Him to be—my own custom-designed God. What I liked, I ascribed to Him; what I didn't like, I ignored. Like an author creating a character in a novel, I crafted a God who could serve my purposes and make all my dreams come true. I knew I had to keep up my end of the bargain, but I fully intended to do everything in my power to please Him and thereby position myself to receive His bountiful blessings—physical, spiritual, financial, social. I only needed the faith to believe, the will to obey, and it would all fall into place. I had developed a "get from God" mentality.

Years later, I came to the inescapable conclusion not only did I have odd-shaped props, but my thoughts were jumbled and knotted. Many and varied light and dark threads of powerful sermons, dramatic stories and illustrations, as well as real-life examples had been introduced into my impressionable mind. Instead of a beautiful pattern emerging as I followed the Christian path, I gazed at a tangled skein. Something was wrong. Christianity did not work the way I had anticipated. Despite my strenuous efforts, I had failed to find the formula to unlock God's storehouse of blessings. Who was at fault? God, me, the teaching I had received, or my application of that teaching?

I recalled the days when I sat at Grandmother Connie's feet and patiently worked at untangling her knitting wool while her needles clicked above me. With intense concentration, I separated each strand. It took time, it took effort, it took discipline, but I recalled the feeling of satisfaction as I wound the untangled wool into a neat ball.

Unraveling the knots in my thinking would require the same commitment. But I had determined to resolve in my mind the authenticity of Christianity. My plodding tenacity kicked in. I would stay the course.

POINTER: Look for Knots in Your Thinking

- Was your religious upbringing filled with "dos and don'ts"?

- Do you see any parallel in what you have read to the way your ideas about God were formed? If so, make a note of these.

- Can you pinpoint and prioritize the concepts that most influenced your thinking?

- Is some untangling of the knots necessary?

POINTER REFLECTIONS:

PART THREE

THE MASTER DESIGNER'S BLUEPRINT

8
BACK TO BASICS

*Seek the L*ORD *your God, and you will find Him if you search for Him with all your heart and all your soul.*
                                        Deuteronomy 4:29 (NASB)

Since the first day that you set your mind to gain understanding and to humble yourself before your God, your words were heard.
                                        Daniel 10:12 (TNIV)

Simplify! Simplify!

The words echoed in my ears. It dawned on me the God I had created in my mind was primarily a hearsay God. For the most part, I had adopted the beliefs of my grandparents and parents without question. Their interpretation of scriptural truth had been corroborated by numerous preachers and missionaries. But instead of resting on a solid foundation, I struggled to hang on to the flimsy pieces of wood and sheetrock that constituted my inherited belief system—before the structure crumbled.

A thousand voices resonated through the chambers of my memory. Each voice, with a differing instruction, was like a wave that further eroded the sand under my shaky, unstable props.

"This is the right way."

"No, this is the right way."

"Here is truth."

"Yes, but that's not all the truth."

"Develop a new attitude."

"God is everywhere. You can't know Him; He's unfathomable."

"God is real. You can know Him."

I needed a new framework. More importantly, I needed a solid foundation.

My thoughts were drawn like a magnet back to the Sinai desert, Moses, and the Israelites. I sensed the Israelites' journey from slavery to freedom held significant clues as to God's identity. There was nothing flimsy about Moses' relationship with God. It was robust and certain, as well as being frank and open. On a dry, ordinary mountain something extraordinary had taken place as God revealed Himself and talked with Moses. He became involved in a new way with humans. Perhaps by delving further I could gain insight into His character and the essential messages He wanted to convey.

However, to get an accurate understanding of the big picture, I needed to start my search at the beginning of the story.

Back to the Beginning

The book of Genesis in the Bible chronicles the fascinating lives of four generations of people: Abram (who later became Abraham), Isaac, Jacob, and Joseph. Much more detail is given covering the period of 2090 BC to 1804 BC than is known for the preceding approximately 2,000 years. Yahweh (God) gets involved in an intensely personal way with these men as He shapes and trains them to accomplish His purposes.

Out of the rapidly multiplying population on Earth, Yahweh selects one faithful, but flawed, human to become the test pilot of a radical new way of life. He calls Abraham to leave his familiar surroundings and family and to embark on a journey to an unknown destination. Abraham is introduced into a life of faith and trust in an invisible God, away from the worship of visible pagan gods. What God said to him was more important than what society said about him. As Eugene Petersen states in *Traveling Light*, "He chose to live extravagantly and recklessly by promise rather than cautiously on a guaranteed income from the Chaldean banks. He chose to live the free life."*

I love the Bible's honesty in recording the failures and stumbles of Abraham's family. In spite of their willfulness and wavering, God detected in them His core prerequisite—hearts turned toward Him. Gently but firmly, He taught, chastised, and nurtured them as He revealed His magnificent design for His creation, that of living free in relationship with Him.

By the time of Abraham's great-grandsons, things were going awry. Jacob, their father, had instructed them in the ways of Yahweh, as his father Isaac and Grandfather Abraham had taught him. But inherited

---

*Eugene Peterson, *Traveling Light*, Colorado Springs, CO: Helmers & Howard, 1988, p. 102. Used by permission.

beliefs were not enough to hold them. Idolatry and false prophets crept in. The children intermarried with the Canaanites and became absorbed in a pagan culture. The uniqueness of this remarkable family diminished. A repetition of what had happened with prior generations appeared inevitable as God's creatures turned their backs on Him and pursued their own interests. Jacob still held to his faith, which he had instilled in his son, Joseph. The story of Joseph and how he appeared to be a victim of circumstances beyond his control is one of my Old Testament favorites.

Yahweh's grand plan for the preservation of a unique people with a radical lifestyle unfolded. Severe famine drove Jacob's family to Egypt, where they lived under Joseph's protection. Even more significant, God created the perfect haven for His chosen people. Culturally, it could not have been better. They were socially isolated. The Egyptians were a proud and noble race who regarded the Hebrews as vastly inferior, and there was no likelihood whatsoever of their allowing intermarriage. Under a benevolent Pharaoh, who owed a debt of gratitude to Joseph for his actions in saving the people from starvation, Jacob's family settled into their peasant lifestyle as herders and farmers in the land of Goshen.

The worship traditions of their forefathers were handed down through succeeding generations. But as the decades passed, Yahweh became remote from their everyday lives. The Yahweh who had spoken audibly to Abraham, dealt personally with Isaac and Jacob, and clearly protected Joseph, remained strangely silent. There were no more dreams, visions, or angelic visitors.

Surrounded by Religion and Religious Practices

Centuries slipped away. Life progressed uneventfully as the Hebrews and their herds multiplied and prospered. Inevitably, the practices of the polytheistic religions of Egypt exerted their influence. Those who continued to worship the Yahweh of their forefathers did so out of tradition and ritual. The impact of Egyptian philosophy made inroads in the thinking of the Hebrews. The Hebrew God was distant and inactive; the Egyptian gods were visible and supposedly active. Eugene Peterson describes the culture of the time:

> Egypt was the most religious culture the world had ever seen. All the architecture was religious. All the organization was religious. The motivation for all the building projects was religious. The art was religious. The politics were religious. The Egyptians had an extraordinary intelligence and a well-organized priesthood. Their wisdom was subtle and mature; their learning was immense; their accomplishments remain to this day awesome. Theirs was a religion designed to make things happen: it guaranteed a happy immortality; it controlled (supposedly) the rising and falling of the Nile so that the land would be fertile; it controlled the people's every move so that there would be law and order.*

---

*Eugene Peterson, *Traveling Light*, Colorado Springs, CO: Helmers & Howard, 1988, p. 139. Used by permission.

One day it all changed. A new king came to power in Egypt, one who did not know, or care to learn, about the historic connection between the Hebrews and their adopted land. To the new ruler, the nation of foreigners living among the Egyptians represented a potential threat to his power. The Hebrews had become an imposing presence, and he distrusted their loyalty in the event of war with a neighboring kingdom. On the advice of his council, Pharaoh began limiting the Hebrews' personal freedom. He imposed heavy taxes and recruited the men into forced labor battalions to hew rock in quarries, build roads, and burn bricks. Their efforts would now benefit the government instead of themselves and contribute to the glory of Pharaoh and Egypt.

Life became unbearable as the Hebrews toiled under the whips of the harsh Egyptian taskmasters. Where was the Yahweh of their ancestors? They begged Him to intervene in their plight. Thus began the fascinating drama recorded in the Old Testament books of Exodus, Deuteronomy, Joshua, and the Psalms.

Yahweh Takes Action

Yahweh did intervene. He selected Moses, a Hebrew and the adopted son of Pharaoh's daughter, a man of privilege and education, schooled in the wisdom of the Egyptians, to be their liberator. Moses' impressive leadership qualifications were offset by his position on Pharaoh's "most wanted" list. He had murdered an Egyptian in a fit of anger over the mistreatment of one of the Hebrew slaves. When the crime surfaced, Moses fled Egypt to escape punishment.

His drop in status could not have been more dramatic—Prince of Egypt to sheepherder in a foreign land. For forty years he wandered in the wilderness, leading a solitary life, learning the ways of the desert—the climate, the winds, the birds and animals, where to find water, what was edible and what to avoid. He didn't know it at the time, but he was in a different educational program, as important, yet far more significant than his studies in Egypt. Yahweh planned to merge the experiences of both worlds. By the time God spoke through the burning bush, Moses had become so removed from his past life of splendor that he argued with God about doing the task to which he was being appointed.

Moses returned to Egypt, and he and Aaron, his brother, asked Pharaoh to release the Hebrews that they might go and worship Yahweh in the desert. As a demonstration of the power of Yahweh, Aaron's rod turned into a serpent. Pharaoh's magicians replicated this with their rods, but Aaron's serpent swallowed the others. Despite this sign of things to come, Pharaoh refused their request. Obstinate and defiant, he made life even more intolerable for the Hebrews. By now they wondered about this man Moses, their so-called deliverer.

Then Yahweh set in motion events to demonstrate His power and uniqueness. Over a period of about a year, He sent ten plagues, three cycles of three, and one last devastating plague. Yahweh chose the calamity; Moses dictated the start and end. In each group of three, the first two were announced to Pharaoh, the third happened without warning. Each was designed to demonstrate to all involved that Yahweh controlled the world—not Pharaoh, not the Egyptian gods.

It was like a domino effect, one plague generating another. According to John H. Dobson in *A Guide to Exodus,* "The nine plagues manifest natural phenomena which occur in the Nile valley, and the miraculous element in them is to be found in their timing, intensity and distribution."[13]

The first three plagues were blows against the sacred river god, Nilus. The people owed their existence to the Nile, depending on the annual runoff from spring rain and melting snow for water to irrigate their crops and deposit fertile top soil. The change in color of the Nile could have been the result of heavy rains in East Africa and Ethiopia washing down fine, red soil into the river. K.A. Kitchen adds "The excessive inundation may have brought with it microcosms known as *flagellates* which would redden the river and also cause conditions that would kill the fish."[14] Because of dead and decaying fish in the Nile, the frogs might leave the river, causing the second plague. The flooding of the land would provide breeding places for the mosquitoes and gnats of the third plague.

In the next set of plagues, Yahweh narrowed the focus and made a distinction between the Hebrews and the Egyptians. As the plagues increased in intensity and severity, the area of Goshen where the Hebrews lived was spared. In a land where polytheism and magic seemed to be supreme, Yahweh demonstrated to all that the Hebrews were a unique people belonging to and protected by the true God, the One who controlled the land of Egypt.

The subsiding floodwaters of the Nile left the land damp, an ideal breeding ground for the fourth plague—swarms of flies. The fifth plague killed only the Egyptians' cattle. The cause may have been anthrax, a disease passed along by the frogs which died in the fields. In humans it causes boils, the sixth plague.

Still Pharaoh vacillated.

The seventh plague brought the worst hail storm in Egyptian history, stripping trees and beating down everything growing in the fields. Whatever was left after the hail was devoured by an invasion of locusts in the eighth plague. The ninth plague was directed against the worship of Ra, the sun god, who was more important than all other Egyptian gods. Yahweh sent three days of darkness so thick it was palpable, clearly demonstrating His superiority.

The overriding control surrounding each plague got the attention of Pharaoh, the magicians, and the Egyptians. Nonetheless, Pharaoh stubbornly refused to let the Hebrews leave, prompting the ultimate blow. Yahweh instructed Moses to tell his people that each household was to select a year-old lamb, slay it at twilight on the fourteenth day of the New Moon, then sprinkle the blood on the doorposts and lintels of their homes. The sprinkled blood would be a sign that Yahweh's destructive force should pass over the occupants. The people were told to cook and eat the slain lamb that night. It was the institution of Passover, observed by devout Jews to this day.

On a single calamitous night, every Egyptian first-born child died, from Pharaoh's, through the members of his court, to the lowliest prisoner languishing in the dungeon. This last plague was an indictment against all Egyptian gods, as the firstborn son of the Pharaoh was regarded as divine. A grief-stricken Pharaoh told Moses to take the people and get out of his sight.

As Yahweh had promised, the blood on the door-posts protected the Hebrews. Gathering their families, possessions, and flocks, they headed out behind Moses on their journey from slavery to freedom.

The Ups and Downs of Freedom

I could imagine the jubilation among the procession of people. The Yahweh of their fathers Abraham, Isaac, and Jacob was back. They had sat around fires listening to tales about the lives of these ancestors, reveling in the dramatic accounts of Yahweh's mighty interventions.

Jubilation dissolved into panic when attention in the camp turned to the cloud of dust on the horizon—caused by hundreds of chariots filled with hostile Egyptians. Pharaoh had reneged on his agreement. With no slave labor force, how could he build edifices for the glory of Egypt and himself? He amassed his army and set off to recapture the Hebrews. The terrified people cried out to Moses: "Is it because there were no graves in Egypt that you have taken us away to die in the wilderness? Why have you dealt with us in this way, bringing us out of Egypt? ... For it would have been better for us to serve the Egyptians than to die in the wilderness."[15]

The man who said he represented Yahweh had misled them, and now they faced dying by the Egyptians' swords. The people were unaware this was the first of thousands of lessons in learning to trust an invisible God.

But Moses told the people "Do not fear! Stand by and see the salvation of the LORD which He will accomplish for you today; for the Egyptians whom you have seen today, you will never see them again forever."[16]

Yahweh again intervened. A mysterious fog enveloped the Hebrews, hiding them from their pursuers. Then Moses stood at the edge of the Sea of Reeds and held out his staff. Nothing extraordinary happened, except the wind picked up. The next morning they discovered the night's strong east wind had created walls of water on either side of a sandy path—an escape route! Later, from the other bank, they watched the Egyptians flounder in confusion, their chariot wheels mired in the damp ground. Then Moses stretched out his staff again, and the waters crashed back to normal level.

The people were thrilled at Yahweh's acts of protection and preservation. When Moses summoned them, they willingly gathered to sing praises to Yahweh for His superior might. A God who could perform spectacular demonstrations of power as they had witnessed over the past year would certainly be able to smooth the way ahead. Life would be good. Optimism soared. They were finally free.

They didn't realize that school had just begun. And they couldn't possibly know they would become alumni for one lonely, hurting woman who, centuries later, would enroll in the same course.

POINTER: It's a Journey—Not a Video Game

- Slaves don't become skilled warriors overnight. There is much to learn, and it takes time.

- Have you been guilty of expecting God to act according to your dictates and wishes?

- Did you feel abandoned when He did not come through?

- Have you complained about the obstacles and inexplicable difficulties in your path?

We will journey with the Hebrew slaves as they move from Egypt, through the wilderness, to freedom in the land God promised them. Open your mind to share in the lessons they, and I, learned along the way.

POINTER REFLECTIONS:

9
THE EQUAL-ARM BALANCE MODEL

You shall love the Lord your God with all your heart, and with all your soul, and with all your mind. [. . .]
You shall love your neighbor as yourself.

Matthew 22:37, 39 (NASB)

Back in the dark ages when I started working in an office, there were no electronic postal scales. The only means we had of calculating postage was an updated version of the ancient equal-arm balance, devised by the Egyptians around 2500 BC. It had a central column supporting a balancing bar. Suspended from one end of the bar was a flat pan big enough to hold an envelope. Suspended on the other end was another pan, which could hold weights in half-ounce increments. We placed the envelope on one pan and then added weights to the other pan until we achieved a balance. Multiplying the combined weight by the current postage rate determined the stamps needed. As soon as the weights were removed, the scale tilted. When both the weights and the envelope were lifted, the scale leveled in preparation for the next item.

Playing with the postage scale, I learned how the precise placement of the crossbar on the central column was essential to its operation. The weights in each pan had to be comparable for accurate measurement. The Western legal system adopted this symbol to represent fairness and order.

Without realizing it, I absorbed the concept of balance.

The Lessons Begin

My study of the Hebrews' path revealed how Yahweh crafted each stage, each event to teach the people about Himself and His ways. He promised Moses He would be with them on their journey, to provide and protect. A pillar of cloud by day and a pillar of fire by night signified His presence. God made ample provision for their failings and weaknesses by instituting animal sacrifices as a tangible act of seeking forgiveness. In return, Yahweh asked that they worship Him as the one true God and obey His commands.

Time passed, and a pattern emerged. The people were having a difficult time on this new path of freedom. When Yahweh demonstrated His power or gave the people some miraculous provision, they vowed they would do everything He asked of them. Then the next hardship came along, and they lost faith, slipping into their predictable habit of whining.

Three months after the Israelites left Egypt, Yahweh announced He would come down to Mount Sinai and talk with Moses within earshot of the people. They were getting restive and dissatisfied with Moses' leadership. The plan wasn't going the way they had dreamed. This God who spoke with Moses was terrifying, not comforting. He issued strange commands. He was unpredictable. They had suffered severe thirst. The food supply, while miraculous in its provision, was hardly appetizing. Its very name, manna, meant "What is it?" and they had to work at collecting it. Moses was not the deliverer they had hoped he would be.

The people had two days to wash their clothes in preparation. On the morning of the third day, they were greeted with thunder and lightning, a thick cloud covered the mountain, and the eerie blast of a trumpet came out of nowhere. Moses led his procession of terrified followers out of the camp and gathered them at the foot of the mountain where, at a safe distance, they mutely watched the strange proceedings. Then Moses spoke, and the voice of God answered, beckoning him to climb the smoking, convulsing mountain.

Moses disappeared into the thick darkness to meet with Yahweh. "When the LORD finished speaking to Moses on Mount Sinai, he gave him the two tablets of the covenant law, the tablets of stone inscribed by the finger of God."[17] Yahweh, Himself, was the author and scribe of what we know as The Ten Commandments:

1. Trust God only.
2. Worship God only.

3. Use God's name in ways that honor Him.
4. Rest on the Sabbath day and think about God.
5. Respect and obey your parents.
6. Protect and respect human life.
7. Be true to your husband or wife.
8. Do not take what belongs to others.
9. Do not lie about others.
10. Be satisfied with what you have.

The first four commandments governed relationship to God. The remaining six addressed relationships to other people.

One day, hundreds of years after Moses, a lawyer challenged Jesus as to his understanding of Mosaic Law. Jesus ingeniously distilled the commandments to: "'You shall love the LORD your God with all your heart, and with all your soul, and with all your mind.' This is the great and foremost commandment. The second is like it, 'You shall love your neighbor as yourself.'"[18]

Same Old, Same Old?

The scenes of lightning, a convulsing mountain, eerie trumpet blasts, and terrified people faded from my imagination. The fascination of the story had again gripped me, but it frankly held no earth-shattering revelation. I was as familiar with "love the Lord your God . . ." as with my ABCs. The idea of putting God first, others next, and self last had been rooted in my psyche. Yet, despite my strenuous efforts, the formula had failed.

Obviously, I had misinterpreted the meaning or missed some key element.

What relevance did ancient Jewish Law have to life in the twenty-first century? How could it illuminate my understanding of God? Jesus believed it important enough to reiterate hundreds of years later. Was Jesus' summary the core message God wanted to convey to His ultimate creation, represented by the Hebrews? Evidently there was significance in this statement that needed further investigation. I studied the meaning of key words.

We all know the heart as the chief organ of physical life. Once the pump stops, life is over. It occupies the most important place in the human system.

Heart symbols are everywhere in our society. We see "I love my Pet" on bumper stickers; Valentine's Day generates hearts by the thousands in cards, balloons, and candy boxes. "Heart" has come to represent a sweetly idealistic version of love. I discovered it is so much more in scripture.

"Heart" was used figuratively for the hidden springs of an individual's personal life, like a pump that generated emotional energy. Used broadly, it encompassed the emotions, the reason, and the will. The word also had huge moral significance in the Old Testament.[19]

The "soul" was described as the immaterial, invisible part of humans, the place where personality resided. Perceiving, reflecting, feeling, desiring, all stemmed from the soul. It also represented the seat of will and purpose.[20]

"Mind" covered all of an individual's conscious experiences—remembering and thinking, intellect and intelligence related to the mind. It housed the faculties of perception and understanding. The mind judged situations and determined a course of action.

What God required of the Israelites, then, was not some gushy sentimental acknowledgment of Him on high days and holidays. He asked that they love Him with everything they were. He wanted a preeminent position in their lives. He wanted to be their only God.

The Master Designer's Blueprint?

In issuing the Ten Commandments, had God revealed the Master Designer's blueprint, a model for humans to become spiritually developed, emotionally whole, and psychologically integrated? The idea appealed to me, but if this were indeed the case, how could I transfer this concept into practical modern living?

A picture of the equal-arm balance flashed onto the screen of my mind. The essential elements of God's instructions connected with its components. I envisioned the support column as representing God. One pan represented relationships with others; the second pan my relationship with myself. The crossbar connecting the separate pieces was my will. I knew from watching my little postal scale that the stability of the central column and the precise placement of the crossbar kept the two pans in a suspended state of balance. The picture communicated stability and fulfillment of purpose.

This arrangement was a far cry from the reality of my life. I had designed my own model. My will became the supporting column, with God as the crossbar, obliged to keep my life in balance according to my desires and dictates. The pan of my needs tilted perilously, depending upon whether the motor of my emotions drove me inward to self-absorption or outward to get my needs met through others. The pan of relationships shifted correspondingly. I was like a weightlifter with too-heavy weights. My knees buckled as I strained to lift the bar, keep the weights in balance, and prevent the whole thing from crashing down on me. The picture conveyed heroic effort, vein-popping strain, and nerve-jangling tension. No wonder I was tired!

The contrasting model intrigued me. What would happen were I to scrap my design and explore the Master design? The model of the equal-arm balance offered a tangible image from which to begin constructing the framework of a new basis for relating to God, others, and myself. Like Moses at the burning bush, I resolved to turn aside and investigate the matter further. I would begin by reevaluating my concept of God, the support column.

POINTER: Keep This Idea in Mind as We Look at Each Component

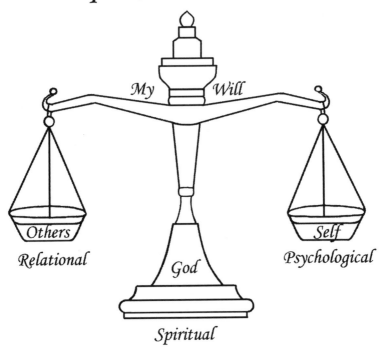

The Equal-Arm Balance Model

Love the LORD your God with all your heart and with all your soul and with all your mind. [. . .] Love your neighbor as yourself.
Matthew 22:37, 39

- Do you think the reality of your life fits or contradicts this model for integrated living?

- Who, or what, comprises your "support column?"

- How would your will function on the model?

POINTER REFLECTIONS:

PART FOUR

THE SUPPORT COLUMN: GOD

10

GOD ABOVE AND AROUND ME

He who made the Pleiades and Orion, and changes deep darkness into morning, Who also darkens day into night, Who calls for the waters of the sea and pours them out on the surface of the earth, The LORD is His name.

Amos 5:8 (NASB)

...the LORD your God, He is God in heaven above and on earth beneath.

Joshua 2:11 (NASB)

I had never struggled over believing in a Supreme Being or even accepting that God brought the universe into existence and shaped the planet we call Earth. Scientists and astronomers told me there was arrangement and harmony in space, the stars and planets were not strewn haphazardly. Each picture transmitted from the Hubble satellite brought a new surge of wonder at the vastness and complexity of the galaxies. Contrasted with such magnitude was the minuteness of microorganisms, equally complex and just as orderly.

Neither did I agonize over whether God literally created the world in seven days, as we know days, or the exact details of the process. There were mysteries the finite human mind would never unravel. I believed science supported the Biblical account of creation; it was human interpretation of the facts that caused conflict.

Scripture stated: "And without faith it is impossible to please God, because anyone who comes to him must believe that he exists and that he rewards those who earnestly seek him."[21] So I chose to begin building my framework of understanding on the foundational assumption that God existed.

Constructing an Image of God

Difficulties arose when I tried to construct an image of the invisible God. I had formed my concept of the character of God by the conclusions I drew from whether and how God answered prayers—mine and those of others. Numerous positive testimonies in Sunday morning church services solidified my belief in a responsive God. When bad things happened in the world, I retreated into a blank space in my mind where I didn't have to deal with the issue. As a result, my "Santa Claus/Genie in a Bottle" thinking had contributed to my creating a faulty image, an unreal deity.

To my sensitive nature, God appeared as an over-exacting tyrant, while to those less sensitive He seemed to remain a comfortable "voice within" who seldom interfered with their pleasure. Although I would never verbalize the word "tyrant" in reference to God, deep down I felt He placed unrealistic demands on me, expecting me to measure up to impossible standards of attitude and behavior.

I knew a lot *about* God, but I now wanted to get to know the real God. The Yahweh who instigated the plan to free His people from slavery. The God who designed a life of freedom, living in relationship with Him.

The Quest Begins

My study of the story of the Exodus had revealed the integral messages that God wanted to communicate to the people He had chosen and called "the Israelites." He wanted them to understand there was only one true God. That He was a God who came near to people, He made Himself known. He had a purpose for humans, and He made that purpose known to them. He was active in the world that He had made. He was God of the past, the present, and the future.

This knowledge, while valuable, was too theoretical, too historical. I had learned from childhood the stories of God's *ways*, but I needed something to reveal the *character* of the Creator. God's dealings with an ancient people were as remote to me as Mars. Had His purposes changed? Had *He* changed?

This was a case for Detective "Determined" Wooderson. I imagined I received an assignment to find someone who had mysteriously disappeared. However, my client refused to give me any information about her missing person—no description, no character trait information, no former residence, no details on habits or hangouts, no aliases, no DNA evidence, etc. I only had a name and instructions to find the individual. It would be the nightmare version of *Without A Trace*—an impossibility.

Fortunately, God must have realized the same thing. He provided a reference source through the inspired record of the ancient writers. Archaeologists continue to discover excavations that support Biblical history.

Despite this, I remember complaining to my mother that so much of the Bible remained incomprehensible.

"Think about it this way," she said. "Supposing you sat down to a meal, and when your plate appeared, on it lay a whole fish—scales, eyes, fins, everything. You'd recoil in horror. But then you found out you weren't expected to eat the whole thing. You'd pick up your knife and fork and begin to dissect the fish, cutting off the eyes and fins, removing the exterior scales, working around the bones, and getting to the good flesh underneath the covering. When you were finished, your plate would hold a mound of unpalatable parts, but you would feel nourished by what you had been able to eat."

I decided to go after the "fish" and leave the bones. The Bible provided a context and related specific incidents of God's dealings with humans. Would it give insight into who He is? Detective Determined purposed to explore, step by step, what God revealed about Himself in scripture.

A Trinity

I understood God made Himself known in three distinct ways: as God the Father, God the Son, and God the Holy Spirit. Not three Gods, but one triune God, revealed in three ways. This concept eluded me until I read St. Augustine of Hippo's comments. He maintained there were many Trinitarian structures within the created universe:

> There is trinity of sight, for example: the form seen, the act of vision, and the mental attention which correlates the two. These three, though separable in theory, are inseparably present whenever you use your sight. Again, every thought is an inseparable trinity of memory, understanding, and will.[22]

Although the Trinity was a mystery hard to comprehend, every time I blinked I realized its possibility. This told me Christianity was a total package.

I thought back to the halcyon days when I enjoyed the luxury of customizing a new car. I ordered subwoofer speakers, an accent stripe, a spoiler, specific interior and exterior colors. But there came a point where my tastes had to bend to what constituted a vehicle—four wheels, an engine, a body, a steering wheel. To eliminate any of these would have left me with a fancy, unique design of something—but I could not call it a vehicle. It would not function as intended.

To fully understand the character of God, I needed to look at Father, Son, and Spirit.

The Father

My initial research into God the Father's attributes revealed that He:

- Has unlimited power or authority, is all-powerful (Genesis 18:14, Job 42:2, Jeremiah 32:27).
- Has infinite knowledge, knows all things (Psalm 139:1-6, 13-16, Job 37:16).
- Is present in all places at the same time (Proverbs 15:3, Jeremiah 23:23-24).
- Is sovereign, above or superior to all others; chief, supreme in power, rank, or authority (Daniel 4:35).
- Is infinite, lacking limits or bounds; extends beyond measure or comprehension, without beginning or end, is vast; immense (1 Kings 8:27, Psalm 139:7-12).
- Is eternal, existing through all time; everlasting; always true or valid; unchanging (Deuteronomy 32:40).
- Surpasses everything and everyone; is extraordinary, exists apart from the material universe (Isaiah 55:8-9).
- Is holy, spiritually perfect or pure; untainted by evil or sin (Leviticus 19:2, Isaiah 47:4).

As impressive as these attributes were, they implied distance, someone majestic, emotionally removed. I am awed by knowledge of such a being, but cannot conceive of sitting across the table chatting with him. It was like asking me if I knew the President of the United States. I knew *of* him. Biographies told me *about* him. But I didn't *know* him. The President would have to single me out, invest time in building a friendship, and then reveal who the real person was behind the office.

God became less remote when I read that He is also:

- Merciful—having, feeling, or showing mercy; compassionate, lenient (Romans 9:14-16).
- Loving—feeling love, devotion; expressing love (Jeremiah 31:3, 1 John 4:8, Romans 5:8).
- Wise—having the ability to judge and deal with persons and situations rightly, based on a broad range of knowledge, experience, and understanding (Daniel 2:20-22, Job 12:13).
- Faithful—which implies continued, steadfast adherence to a person or thing to which one is bound by an oath, duty, obligation (Deuteronomy 7:9, Lamentations 3:23).
- Truthful—presenting the facts honestly (Titus 1:2, Numbers 23:19).
- Kind—sympathetic, gentle, tenderhearted, generous (Psalm 117:2, Ephesians 2:7).

- Just—fair, equitable, impartial, righteous, upright (Psalm 89:14, Deuteronomy 32:4).

Glimpses into God's Heart

I discovered God added another dimension when He revealed His names, scattered throughout scripture. In Biblical times a name represented a person's character or something significant about them. Moses' first son was named Gershom because this expressed his father's emotions at the time of the child's birth, "I have become an alien in a foreign land."

In the ancient Hebrew text, it was as if God opened His heart to reveal the essence of who He was. He referred to Himself as:

> *Elohim* – The Creator of All Things
> *El Elyon* – God Most High, Sovereign Ruler of the Universe
> *El Roi* – The God Who Sees
> *El Shaddai* – The All-Sufficient One
> *Jehovah* or *Yahweh* – The Self-Existent One
> *Jehovah-jireh* – Provider
> *Jehovah-rapha* – Healer
> *Jehovah-raah* – Shepherd

God became less ethereal as these character attributes implied involvement and action. They were the expressions of a God who wanted to play a significant role in the lives of His people.

But this still left me with an unsolvable problem. How could I, in my human finiteness, connect with an invisible God? I needed a tangible representation. It was time to look at the second person of the Trinity, Jesus, whom the Bible said was the image of the invisible God.[23]

Approximately 2,000 years ago God reached out to humanity in a radical way by putting in motion a plan to offer reconciliation and connection to Himself. He sent his son, Jesus, to live on Earth. Humbling himself, Jesus took on human form and limitations and arrived as a helpless baby in a cattle stall in a Middle Eastern town called Bethlehem.

God moved closer.

POINTER: Spend Time Considering God's Attributes

- Run through the list of God's attributes. Check those you knew about. Mark those which are surprising.

- Which of God's attributes appeal most to you?

- Which would you rather ignore?

- If you met a human with God's attributes, would you want to get to know that person?

- Would you feel intimidated, afraid, awed?

POINTER REFLECTIONS:

11

GOD NEXT TO ME

The Son is the radiance of God's glory and the exact representation of his being, sustaining all things by his powerful word.

Hebrews 1:3 (TNIV)

And He is the image of the invisible God, the first-born of all creation.

Colossians 1:15 (NASB)

On one of my visits to England, my cousin and I spent time in the National Gallery in London. Starting from the basement, we wound our way up through endless corridors and rooms filled to capacity with works of art. The lowest levels featured religious art produced for the Christian Church between the third and seventh centuries. After Emperor Constantine issued an edict making Christianity a state religion of the Roman Empire, artistic activity surged. Wall upon wall held impressions of artists as they wrestled with the visual depiction of the immortal, yet mortal, Christ. I saw numerous pictures of the Madonna and Child, a halo surrounding the baby's head. Gold accents signified his supernatural status. The art was unquestionably beautiful; however, the portrayals bore little relation to the actuality of life in those times. Religious interpretation tainted and clouded reality. The artists presented what the religious leaders and wealthy patrons wanted to see.

I had to acknowledge I had an equally distorted view of Jesus. The Jesus in my mind had stuck on the level of my childhood Sunday School stories. I failed to grasp the paramount importance of his claim to be God.

God Enters the World

Somewhere between 740 and 680 BC, the prophet Isaiah prophesied the birth of Jesus. He explained how God planned for a Messiah to atone for the sin of humans once and for all, thereby making unnecessary the continual blood sacrifices required of the Israelites as a symbol of their repentance.

The Bible stated God made humans in His image, not a physical image, but that humanity bore the stamp of the essence of God—intellect, spirit, will, emotions. To me, the most revealing passage in Isaiah was his proclamation that the baby would be called Immanuel, translated, "God with us." Jesus brought to Earth the character and essence of Almighty God while taking on the form of a man.

If God's plan were announced today and placed in the hands of humans to implement, there would be years of frenzied planning and preparation. Committees would be assigned specific duties, with public relations the most active force as they whipped anticipation to a fever pitch through the media. Pundits speculating about the impending arrival would clog the air waves. The Son of God, founder of the Kingdom of Heaven, was soon to be born on Earth!

Instead, a lusty cry from an infant in a stable announced his arrival. God came, not as a king, nor celebrity, but as a helpless baby, to learn from scratch what it truly was like to be human. But rather than introducing a comforting, sustaining sense of the presence of God on Earth, Jesus initiated a maelstrom of controversy, especially in the religious world of his day.

Focused God—or Lunatic?

For centuries, religious traditions and customs had been the mainstay of Jewish culture. The people thought they understood who God was and what He expected in terms of right conduct. Above all, they knew their Yahweh to be the only God.

Then out of the obscurity of Nazareth, in Galilee, a man emerged who went about saying he was the son of God, that he had power to forgive sins, and that he had always existed with God. C.S. Lewis puts the impact of these actions into perspective:

> Among Pantheists, like the Indians, anyone might say that he was a part of God, or one with God: there would be nothing

very odd about it. But this man, since He was a Jew, could not mean that kind of God. God, in their language, meant the Being outside the world, who had made it and was infinitely different from anything else. And when you have grasped that, you will see that what this man said was, quite simply, the most shocking thing that has ever been uttered by human lips.[*]

There were no talking heads on television in Jesus' day, but I could imagine the heated arguments in the Temple when word got around about his claims. No wonder they called him a blasphemer against Yahweh. Either Jesus was a complete lunatic, or he was indeed focused God. I had a vague childish affection for a half-remembered Jesus, but had never used my adult critical faculties on the matter.

A huge stumbling block for many otherwise honest intellectual people is Jesus' astounding assertion "I am the way and the truth and the life. No one comes to the Father except through me."[24] Such a narrow view runs counter to modern society's popular inclusive thinking. A Supreme Being who is Love would never place such a restriction on His creation. But I wondered, "Why shouldn't He?"

If I were fabulously wealthy and wanted to share my largesse with people, I have the prerogative of determining the parameters within which this would be done: people born on my birthday, AIDS orphans, or

---

[*]*Mere Christianity* by C.S. Lewis, copyright C.S. Lewis Pte. Ltd. 1942, 1943, 1944, 1952. Extract reprinted by permission.

the Humane Society. I get to decide. My family, friends, and business associates might disapprove of my choices; at best I'd be labeled highly eccentric. The topic would cause a flurry of attention on the talk show circuit. But in the end, most people would shrug and say, "It's her money, she can do with it as she likes."

It made sense, then, that a supreme, holy, undefiled God should have the right to make the determination as to how individuals approached Him. His "largesse" is reconciliation with Him, both now and for eternity. He set the parameters.

God With Skin On

This all remained rather abstract until one night at an Easter play the historical figure of Jesus came alive. I saw him from a new perspective—as a human male. The play dramatized several scenes from key events in his life.

I was struck by the depiction of his personality. This was a supremely charismatic man. His easy interaction with men and women sprang from a deep-seated confidence in his identity, a freedom to be himself, to express love and appropriately receive love. He laughed with them. Children ran to him to be picked up and hugged. At the tomb of Lazarus, in front of many people, he expressed grief. He shared in the excitement and joy following a physical healing. He dealt compassionately with the adulterous woman about to be stoned by the exacting religious leaders. He accepted social outcasts and lepers and elevated the status of women. Jesus was an appealing person, enigmatic and controversial, but a leader to be admired and followed. His was an integrated, emotionally whole personality.

The humanity of Jesus touched me. I began to compare the character, actions, and attitudes of Jesus with what I knew about the attributes of God.

Jesus stated his purpose was to reflect God the Father's character and to teach humans how to live in a new spiritual dimension—the Kingdom of God. His "I AM" statements recorded in the Gospel of John revealed his desire to meet hidden longings and needs in human hearts: guidance, security and care, freedom from distorted thinking, adventurous living, hope, joy, comfort in grief and pain.[25]

The aloof God of the Old Testament had become approachable. Christianity held out the offer of a love relationship with the Deity, the unmerited favor of the Creator of the universe.

I decided to do an Internet search on the word "love" in the Bible. Its derivative, "loving kindness," was one of the most important terms in the vocabulary of Old Testament theology and ethics. The meaning in the Hebrew word encompasses three English words: strength, steadfastness, and love. In the New Testament it takes on the added meaning of "grace." The Bible was full of references about God's love toward humankind. Further, God's love was shown to be unselfish and unmerited—initiated by Him toward His creatures. His only stipulation was that humans come to Him via Jesus.

Although Jesus set aside his deity, he remained the Son of God, destined to break through the barrier separating a holy God and humans, to bring about reconciliation and forgiveness for the rest of time. Jesus would experience death—but triumph over it. He introduced the concept of God's love in a new way to the people on Earth.

How bleak those three days Jesus lay in the grave must have been for his followers. If he were the Son of God, why was he lying in a borrowed tomb? His close disciples scattered, fearing for their lives. Confusion reigned. It all seemed so pointless. They'd given their loyalty to someone who in the crisis couldn't measure up to his claims, a mortal man with no more power than any other radical leader. Then came the Resurrection.

I recently visited the Continental Divide at the summit of Berthoud Pass in the Rockies, where a drop of water is directed in one of two directions, to the Atlantic or the Pacific Oceans. For the first time, I grasped how Jesus' resurrection served as the "Continental Divide" in the religious world, the point at which Christianity separated from all other religions. Jesus was not merely a charismatic man with revolutionary ideas. He fulfilled the ancient prophecies and ratified his claim to be the Son of God.

Those who believed in him became the spark that ignited the flame of Christianity. However, Jesus anticipated that without his physical presence to encourage, teach, and protect them, it was unlikely his followers would maintain their commitment to this radical new way of living.

So God implemented the next step in the plan. He moved even closer—He moved *in*!

Up to this point, my beliefs concurred with what I had been taught and with what my grandparents and parents believed. The birth, death, and resurrection of Jesus constituted the essentials of the Christian faith.

But now I faced the most confusing aspect of the Triune God—the Spirit.

POINTER: Spend Time Reviewing Your Thoughts About Jesus

- What do you think about Jesus, his life and ministry?

- Can you accept that he was more than a baby in a manger, as depicted on Christmas cards—that he came to earth to be God with us, or God with skin on?

- Have you considered that Jesus really *was* the expression of God's love to the humans He created?

- Consider the implications of this . . .

POINTER REFLECTIONS:

12
GOD IN ME?

And I will ask the Father, and He will give you another Helper, that He may be with you forever; that is the Spirit of truth, whom the world cannot receive, because it does not behold Him or know Him, but you know Him because He abides with you, and will be in you.

John 14:16, 17 (NASB)

I once heard a story about a little girl who protested loudly to her parents that she no longer wanted to go to church. Her parents could not understand her surprising resistance. Finally, her father asked the reason.

"I'm afraid to go to church!" she blurted out.

"Why on earth are you afraid?" probed her father.

"I don't want to go to church because I am afraid of the Holy Ghost that my Sunday School teacher told me about!"

This story illustrates a profound reality. I believe there is more misunderstanding over the purpose and work of the Holy Spirit than anything else in the Bible.

Opinion runs the full gamut. Reputable theologians who agree to disagree on many unclear topics become dogmatic and strident on the subject of the operation of the Spirit. The Deceiver, Satan, sees to it that the confusion and controversy are multiplied. After all, if you want to render something useless, attack the power source!

The Bible states that the Spirit's primary purpose is to make the teachings of Jesus real in the hearts of believers and to empower them to live as his representatives.

Rampant Confusion

Reflecting on my past experience growing up in a Pentecostal environment, I pictured a line with the number one at the beginning and the number ten at the opposite end. One represented the people who paid absolutely no attention to the Holy Spirit; they were ignorant of His role or they chose to ignore Him. At the opposite end were the folks whom we call the "holy rollers." Below the mid-point were the many people who had intellectual knowledge of the Spirit, and each week, as part of church liturgy, made mention of him. Above mid point were those who placed tremendous emphasis on the Holy Spirit. Their worship could be highly emotional, with frequent demonstrations of the "sign gifts," such as speaking in tongues, interpretation, and prophecy.

I became aware at an early age of the operation of the "sign gifts" in some services simply by attending Dad's church. Sometimes my father or mother would give a "message in tongues," and someone else would give an understandable interpretation. A holy hush fell over the congregation. The message came across as pertinent and relevant, and I had a strong sense that what I observed and heard was authentic.

Other times, however, the messages given by certain people didn't ring true. I questioned my parents about this. They explained that an individual's human nature can get in the way of the leading of the Spirit. That sometimes people may try to impress others with their spirituality, and that there are occasions when the actions are simply out of order.

Each year we attended Youth Camp. After the evening service, the leader gave an invitation for folks to spend time in prayer seeking the Baptism in the Spirit. This was for those who desired the ultimate connection with God, confirmed by the supernatural occurrence of speaking in an unknown tongue. Many stayed behind to pray. I accepted that seeking "the Baptism" was probably the right thing to do, but fear of embarrassment restrained me. There were times when I went forward for prayer. But nothing happened; no supernatural power came upon me. My reserved, retiring nature struggled against the exuberance and demonstrations of the experience others were having.

The next day there would be great excitement because so-and-so had "spoken in tongues" and "received the Baptism." All who had experienced a similar encounter gathered around the individual. The rest of us stood and mutely watched. I felt left out of this "exclusive club" whose members obliquely conveyed a sense of spiritual superiority.

Testimonies from the "Baptized folks"—about increased boldness in sharing their faith, an awareness of more power in prayer, and a growing desire for God's Word—caused even greater confusion. I concluded I could not enjoy a similar level of boldness, power, or desire for the Word of God without having this experience.

Hand-Me-Down Beliefs

Grandpa Archie adamantly held that the Baptism of the Spirit was a separate experience from receiving Christ as Savior. It was a superior, much-to-be-desired next step in spiritual growth made available to those who were truly "sanctified," or who had achieved a higher level of holiness.

While my parents taught me it was all right to apply discernment in this area, my questioning remained tentative and peripheral. Who was I to challenge the theological teaching of a Pentecostal founder? To doubt the "operation of the Spirit" would, in my mind, have bordered on heresy. So I stifled my reservations. Neither Mom nor Dad ever said anything directly about my not being a "true Pentecostal." I just floundered on the edge of the spiritual action. Eventually, I put the subject on the back burner of my mind as being entirely too confusing.

A Different View

Almost thirty years passed, and I heard a different teaching. It was quite revolutionary to me—but it made sense.

Study confirmed the doctrinal truth that the Spirit takes up residence in a person upon acceptance of Jesus

Christ as Savior. From that moment on, power, strength, wisdom—and everything else—becomes available to the believer. Whether this is actually appropriated in an individual's life is an independent, personal decision.

Living in an agrarian society, Jesus often used vegetation to illustrate a point he wanted to make. To explain this profound truth, he drew attention to a vine and its branches. The branch connected to the vine looked healthy and growing, with the potential of bearing fruit in its season. The branch on the ground lay withered and lifeless. Jesus then stated he was the vine; his followers were the branches. The sap running from the vine through the branches represented the Holy Spirit. The branches had to remain attached to the vine in order to enjoy the life-giving sap.[26]

My mind drifted to the tree in the backyard of our home in subtropical Durban. It never quite lost all its leaves. Consequently, at certain times of the year we looked out on a tree bursting with new life, while scraggly old leaves clung to the branches. Someone joked to Dad that perhaps we should mount an all-out assault on the tree and pull off the dead leaves to make way for the new. Wisely, he replied, "Don't worry about the old leaves. The thrust of the new life will eventually push them off the tree."

What a wonderfully simple arrangement. It took away all sense of striving. The new life came from within, and its force brought about external changes. The power of the Spirit produced love, joy, peace, patience, kindness, goodness, faithfulness, gentleness, and self-control.[27] These qualities were the "fruit" of the Spirit who worked in a person's heart, mind, and will. God could do in me what I could not do for myself—a liberating, mysterious concept.

A Solid, Adequate Support Column

My childish, inherited view of God was being replaced with a more accurate picture. God was no longer the distant deity who kept raising the bar with His performance expectations. He was my Creator, who reached out in love to me, His creature, from the beginning. Jesus, the Son, was the expression of that love. The Spirit was Christ's presence in me, available to empower me to live as God designed. This God was the one whom I was commanded to love with all my heart, soul, and mind.

I was beginning to get the first inkling of the inherent strength in my support column. The challenge of translating beliefs into behavior lay ahead.

And that led to the next component of my model— the complex role of my will.

POINTER: Reflect on Jesus' Illustration of the Vine and the Branches

- What is your understanding of the Spirit of God? A "ghost?" A strange "force?" Something to be feared and avoided?

- Does the concept of God for me, God with me, God in me, cast new light on your understanding of the Trinity?

- Does the idea of being a "branch" connected to the "vine" and allowing the life-giving "sap" to flow through offer hope for change?

- If so, what about you would you like to see changed?

POINTER REFLECTIONS:

PART FIVE

THE CROSSBAR: HUMAN WILL

13

IT'S MY CHOICE

*But if serving the L*ORD *seems undesirable to you, then choose for yourselves this day whom you will serve.*

Joshua 24:15 (TNIV)

Our wills are ours, we know not how; our wills are ours, to make them Thine.

—Tennyson

I've always admired visionaries who dare to pursue a dream, whether it is starting a business, ballooning over the Atlantic, or finishing college at age seventy. Conversely, I recoil in horror at atrocities committed by despots. The motivating force in each instance is the power of human will.

According to C. S. Lewis:

> God created things which had free will. That means creatures which can go either wrong or right. [. . .] If a thing is free to be good it is also

free to be bad. And free will is what has made evil possible. Why, then, did God give them free will? Because free will, though it makes evil possible, is also the only thing that makes possible any love or goodness or joy worth having.[*]

The Creator gave humans a unique gift—the ability to reason, explore options, and make decisions, unlike other creatures who follow a herd instinct. While God knew what would happen if His creatures used their wills the wrong way, He apparently thought it worth the risk. He could have created automatons, compliant robots that would never be aggravating, would worship on call, and do His bidding without question. But God wanted voluntary love and fellowship. He desired that His ultimate creatures come willingly to Him, not under coercion or out of obligation, so He placed no limitations on human will except the warning voice of conscience.

I had never given much thought to the role of my will, probably because I drifted along in a limbo-land of wishing and waiting for God to perform the miracle I wanted. I knew how to exercise my will when it came to saving for an overseas trip or a new sports car. But anything beyond that got lost in the fog of confusion surrounding "God's will." What was left of my own will had been trampled on and almost annihilated by my bulldozer emotions.

In her classic *A Christian's Secret of a Happy Life*, Hannah Whittall Smith gives a concise explanation of the role of human will. She believed the will is the governing

---

[*]*Mere Christianity* by C.S. Lewis, copyright C.S. Lewis Pte. Ltd. 1942, 1943, 1944, 1952. Extract reprinted by permission.

power in an individual's nature, the action generator. It's that independent self that makes decisions and controls everything, separate from our emotions.

There is an amazing verse in the book of Revelation that provides insight into the Creator's respect for the supremacy of the human will: "Here I am! I stand at the door and knock. If anyone hears my voice and opens the door, I will come in and eat with them, and they with me."[28] The speaker is resurrected Jesus, addressing his disciple, John.

William Hunt masterfully captured this message in his painting, "The Light of the World." He depicted the figure of Jesus standing outside a door. In one hand he holds a lantern; the other hand is raised as if knocking on the door. The remarkable aspect of the picture is the missing outside door handle. The Son of God, who spoke the world into existence, will not gatecrash my life. He gave me freedom of will at conception; he will not usurp that freedom. He initiates and reaches out; I choose whether to respond.

For the first time, I opened my mind to the profound significance of the unique gift God gave me— free will, the capacity to do good or evil, the ability to make choices. As a child, I had "given my heart to Jesus" and had somehow misunderstood or been misled into thinking that as a Christian my will was no longer mine. Wrong! My will is mine until the day I draw my final breath. The issue is what I do with it.

How, then, could I reconcile freedom of will, given to me by God, with His command in the Hebrew Law to love Him with all my heart, soul, and mind? In modern Western society, the idea of loving by decree is ludicrous. I might be compelled to obey some authority figure, but nobody can force me to love.

A.W. Tozer shed light on my dilemma. He contended there are two kinds of love: the love of feeling and the love of willing. The one lies in the emotions, the other in the will. The love the Bible commands is not the love of feeling; it is the love of willing.[29]

My efforts to muster feelings of love for God proved erratic. I felt waves of gratitude when life progressed smoothly; I struggled against an avalanche of doubt when it did not. The "love of willing" called for deliberate, purposeful action. It implied a profound level of trust, which I found frightening. I discovered that my struggle was merely a twenty-first century recounting of the struggle of the Israelites.

Who's in Charge?

The issue of who was in control was a dominant theme in the ancient saga. Yahweh offered to be the Hebrews' God, to provide care and guidance on their journey, and to fulfill His promise to turn Abraham's descendants into a great nation. In return, He asked the people to relinquish any attachment to Egyptian idols and worship only Him. It sounded straightforward and simple.

The people acknowledged that Yahweh had demonstrated His superiority over the Egyptian gods. Further, He had miraculously provided for their basic needs of food and water. They wanted to learn and enjoy this new life of freedom. When Moses challenged them to obey God's commands, they responded, "We will do everything the LORD has said."[30] Such a God was certainly worthy of their obedience and worship.

Moses went back up the mountain to report their answer to God—and stayed away too long. The people got tired of hanging around the camp and wanted to move on to the Promised Land. Up to this point, Yahweh had led them step by step through the wilderness by a pillar of cloud or fire. When it moved, they moved. When it stayed, they stayed. Now nothing was happening. Boredom set in.

They didn't realize the emptiness was a crucial step on this new path of freedom. The people began to make demands. They wanted Aaron, Moses' brother and co-leader, to make them a visible god since they had no idea what had become of Moses. "They did not want to live in response to God but wanted gods that they could use to get what they wanted, like they had had in Egypt—gods one could move around and use to make things happen."*

Aaron had a choice. Perhaps he reasoned that the people weren't exactly turning their backs on Yahweh, they only wanted an Egyptian god as well. What harm could there be in that? Aaron succumbed to their request. Melting their golden earrings, he fashioned a calf like the bull god, Apis. Then Aaron, Moses' right-hand man and a member of his inner circle, led the people in worship to a pagan god. Past programming overcame him.

The Bible records God's anger at this deliberate violation of His command to worship no one other than Himself. Despite their actions, Yahweh allowed the people to exercise their free will one more time. They were told to choose whom they wanted as their God.

---

*Eugene H. Peterson, *Traveling Light,* Colorado Springs, CO: Helmers & Howard, 1988, p. 142. Used by permission.

As always, there were consequences, and many of those who turned against Yahweh died. The elements that bred distrust of God's and Moses' leadership had to be removed.

I felt immense gratitude that I did not have to deal with the fearsome God of the Old Testament. No doubt I would have been obliterated long ago. Yet I had to look beyond God's acts of punishment, deeper into the character of the Being behind the acts. This incident was part of the hammering process as Yahweh refashioned and shaped the people. Learning to trust an invisible God was as much a challenge then as it is today. Learning to wait when it appears nothing is happening is an even greater challenge.

It's My Decision

My investigation revealed that God regards the decisions and choices of a woman's will as the decisions and choices of the woman herself, no matter how contrary her emotions may be. The key is to set the will right, and the emotions will follow.

Suddenly it made sense. All I had to do was will to be willing to do the will of God—regardless of how I felt!

I consider myself something of a handyman. I can replace toilet innards, worn out washers, and do minor electrical repairs. I regularly replace the filters in my heating/air-conditioning unit. At the beginning of one winter, I went through the process. After completing the task, I replaced the cover of the unit, turned out the light, and closed the door. It wasn't cold enough to have heat in the home yet.

A couple of weeks later, I felt uncomfortably cool. Alarmed, I checked the setting on the thermostat. All was fine. I played around with the switch. Nothing happened. I peered at the unit, and everything looked in order. I waited for a miracle. None came. My home got progressively colder. In desperation I went again to examine the unit. This time I noticed that the cover did not seem to be properly placed. I maneuvered it around, banged on it, and presto, heat! The cover had to be precisely positioned to deactivate the safety switch.

I thought again of the image of the equal-arm balance. Perhaps in order for us to experience life as God intended, the key building block is the precise placement of the crossbar of human will on the support column. The same way the crossbar of the scale keeps the dual pans in balance, the will keeps the three areas of relationships in balance—with God, others, and ourselves. Too much "heavenly focus" and we become no earthly good. An overemphasis on self makes us self-absorbed. Constant attention to the needs of others puts us out of touch with God and ourselves.

Paging God!

I had spent a lifetime thinking I was trying to align my will with God's will. In fact, to be accurate, I wanted to align God's will with mine. I clung to the verse "No good thing does he withhold from those whose walk is blameless."[31] This hooked into the many stories about "believing God," "expecting from God," "taking God at his word," and a million other exhortations to "exercise faith" for whatever it was I needed or wanted. I have only to turn on my television to the religious channels to hear ardent preachers urging similar action.

To me, faith meant expecting and receiving supernatural intervention in times of need, overcoming obstacles to accomplish God's work, and experiencing miraculous healings and overflowing blessings. The term faith, as in Christian faith, became secondary to this active application of the word. While I had come by this understanding honestly, I didn't grasp the distinction until almost a lifetime later. I realized how I *chose* to focus on what suited me and my wishes.

I had a clear idea of what I thought was good for me, so I paged God. When this elicited no response, I paged again. I imagined God looking at the pager, identifying the caller, and going about His business. He would get back with me at an appropriate time. However, I felt He ignored my request.

The story of a medieval monk described with painful accuracy the pattern of my thinking. He decided he needed oil, so he planted an olive sapling.

"Lord," he prayed, "it needs rain that its tender roots may drink and swell. Send gentle showers." And the Lord sent gentle showers.

"Lord," prayed the monk, "my tree needs sun. Send sun, I pray Thee." And the sun shone, gilding the dripping clouds.

"Now frost, my Lord, to brace its tissues," cried the monk. And soon the little tree sparkled with frost. But at evening it died.

The monk sought out a brother monk and related his experience. "I, too, planted a little tree," he said, "and see, it thrives well. But I entrust my tree to its God. He who made it knows better what it needs than a man like me. I laid no condition. I fixed no ways or means. 'Lord, send what it needs,' I prayed, 'storm or sunshine, wind, rain, or frost. You made it and you know best.'"

The message registered. I wanted God in on *my* agenda! My constant paging was based on my inability to trust His intentions for me. I couldn't trust God's intentions because I didn't know His character.

A wall plaque at Joan's lake cottage stated simply, *"God gives the best to those who leave the choice to Him."*

"All right, God. I don't understand why you've left me without a mate, but I want to trust your wisdom, and I want to believe you desire what is best for me. I'm quitting my insistent paging."

I resolved, like the second monk, to relinquish control and begin trusting the ordering of my circumstances to the One who made me and knows me best. It was a worthy and noble intellectual decision; putting it into practice was another matter entirely.

Setting the Controls of My Will

My love of flying surfaced imagery that connected in my mind. I imagined myself as the pilot of a plane. The passengers were on board, the door was closed, seat belts were fastened, and we were ready to leave the gate. The plane was pushed back and we began taxiing to the runway. Finally, the air traffic controller gave the go ahead for takeoff. I began the acceleration, adjusting the flaps and settings. The huge engines responded, and the aircraft gathered speed. I studied the gauges. I still had the option of aborting the flight and returning to the gate. I was in control of the aircraft. But my desire was for flight, so I held steady on the controls. Then the aircraft reached the point where the law of aerodynamics overrode the law of gravity, and the giant machine lifted from the ground. At that moment, I was committed to flight. There was no turning back.

Like a captain, I needed to set the "controls" of my will toward God. My will touched every aspect of my being and was never at rest. It set the tone of daily existence. How I used the unfathomable power of my free will determined the course of my life. Following the design of the equal-arm balance, I resolved to rest the crossbar of my will firmly on the support column representing God.

Unfortunately, God did not respond to my willingness to submit by applying heavenly glue to cement the pieces. What I now faced was the challenge of maintaining the precise balance of the crossbar on the support column in order to learn to function optimally. Was I looking at more striving, even more effort?

The words of an old hymn offered a liberating, uplifting new slant:

> O to grace how great a debtor
> Daily I'm constrained to be;
> Let Thy goodness, like a fetter,
> Bind my wandering heart to Thee:
> Prone to wander, Lord, I feel it,

Prone to leave the God I love;
Here's my heart, O take and seal it,
Seal it for Thy courts above (italics
mine).[32]

Relief swept over me as I reflected on the beautiful simplicity of God's design. If I voluntarily choose to submit my will (heart) to Him, He takes my offering of trust and places His seal upon it, securing it for eternity. With the crucial components of the support column and the crossbar in place, I am put in the position of learning to function as God intended, in balance with Him, others, and myself.

I wanted to learn to trust an invisible God, to reorganize the framework of my life so that my will was positioned to rest on the support column of His strength and stability.

Like the Israelites, my resolve would be severely tested.

POINTER: Analyze the Role of Your Will

- Have you ever taken time to consider the part your "will" plays in your daily life?

- Were you aware that even God will not violate your free will?

- Think about the idea of resting the crossbar of your will upon the support column of God.

- What would have to change in your thinking, lifestyle?

POINTER REFLECTIONS:

14
TESTING THE THEORY

One doesn't discover new lands without consenting to leave sight of the shore for a very long time.

—André Gide

The Monument to the Explorers in Lisbon, Portugal, towered above me. The sculptor had masterfully captured the sense of adventure that it represented. I gazed at the bow of a ship, thrusting forward, the tall granite in the middle representing a billowing sail. At its tip, the figure of visionary Prince Henry the Navigator held a small sailing ship in his hand. Behind him, carrying flags, charts, sextants, and swords, ranged the figures of the intrepid men who in the fifteenth century ventured into the unknown in ships that bobbed on heaving seas like corks in a bathtub.

Five hundred years later, the images of these men captured my imagination as I stared thoughtfully at them. Known as the greatest patron of discovery, Prince Henry sent out well-organized and ably conducted expeditions from Portugal to explore trading routes to India and the East. These explorers had no idea what lay before them when they left the safe harbor of home. Their journey would take months, even years. Many would never return. One of those men on the freeze above me, Bartolomeu Dias, had first rounded the tip of Africa in 1487. A decade later, Vasco Da Gama steered his battered ship into the tranquil bay of what would one day become the Cape Colony.

Those adventurers risked their lives in their determination to explore the unknown. The challenges were beyond comprehension, yet through their exploits they changed the world. The men depicted on the monument made a choice.

The wistful desire for something more that had lain dormant in me for many years now stirred. I longed for freedom, to escape the shackles of religious traditions. According to Eugene Peterson, "All the great stories of exploration and discovery are parables of Christian venture. Columbus didn't sail across the ocean, decide to create a new continent, go back to Spain and organize a flotilla of ships to bring loads of dirt in order to make the Americas. It was already there. He discovered and explored it."*

I had arrived at the point where theory either remained theory or got translated into action. I could settle back with my remote, intellectual understanding of what I had learned about the Triune God, or I could unlatch the door of my will and see what happened.

---

*Eugene H. Peterson, *Traveling Light,* Colorado Springs, CO: Helmers & Howard, 1988, p.77. Used by permission.

I wanted the miracle-working God to send an angel to touch my head like a fairy godmother. This act would no doubt instantly align my will with God's forever, evaporate all confused thinking, and set me on the path of freedom and wholeness. Instead, He left my free will intact and offered me a choice. Like the early explorers, He called me to venture out of my comfort zone into the unknown, to embark on what would become a lifelong journey of discovery about Him, others, and myself.

The hope of uncharted seas, an unexplored land mass, or secret wealth gave impetus to the explorers. They learned to withstand unimaginable hardships and grasped the meaning of raw, unvarnished endurance. Little did I realize the hope beckoning me forward would require all that of me.

A Dream is Born

It was 1989, during the annual World Missions Conference at my Baptist church in Atlanta. My body sat upstairs in the balcony. My mind drifted 10,000 miles away to Dad's former church in Durban. I saw again the banners with slogans urging involvement in missions. I heard once more the impassioned pleas for the privileged to reach out to those less fortunate, the spiritually lost and physically needy.

Dad organized his church's first mission conference in 1956. Holding such a conference would not be startling in the U.S.A. or Britain, but it was revolutionary in South Africa. The action of a man of courage and faith.

The Afrikaners who took control of the government in 1948 believed they were chosen people, honored by God, destined to enjoy privileged status. To them, the gospel was primarily a "white" message.

By 1956, *apartheid* exerted a strangle hold on all people, creating fear of retribution for anyone holding a differing view. Yet Dad forged ahead with his mission emphasis, ministering to the African people while steering clear of anything that could stir up anti-government activity and draw the attention of the harsh, repressive officials. An ordinary man, he attempted to do something extraordinary by God's power.

Now, pictures that spanned more than thirty years flashed through my mind. I saw dirt-poor African ministers grinning at the luxury of having bicycles for transportation. A district superintendent stood proudly next to a shining Volkswagen Kombi (given to him—along with driving lessons). There were piles of clothes available for distribution to congregations in remote areas. I heard the inimitable sound of African choirs as they sang in natural harmony. The cause of missions had been imprinted on my heart and would never be erased.

The preacher's voice brought me back to the present. "What better way to spend your life than being involved in the extension of God's Kingdom? Those of you who are nearing retirement have the opportunity to devote your remaining years to a cause greater than yourself."

I was stirred, as always. But this time the speaker's comments connected in a new way. The prospect of early retirement from Delta Air Lines was a dot on the horizon. I responded to the sermon's challenge by silently telling God I would like to retire early and become involved in some aspect of mission activity. I told myself I wanted to carry on the tradition of my family. In reality, I searched for meaning. Perhaps if I got involved in something that had "eternal" significance, I would find contentment.

A Call to Risk

Years passed, and life meandered on. Circumstances closed in on me at work. Twelve years of complaining passengers had depleted my store of tact and energy. Turbulence rumbled through the industry and the company. By now I was eligible for early retirement, but financially it was impractical, bordering on foolish. I earned a good salary, had excellent benefits, and was building seniority—which in the airline industry is your most valued asset.

Then one day we were told about forthcoming modifications to Delta's early retirement package. This forced me into making a decision: take what I could get now or plan to stick it out for possibly the next twelve years. In my view, this was a much scarier step than getting married. Marriage was revocable. Retirement was not. I stared again at the financial figures, which showed no sign of improving, and told my colleagues they would have the pleasure of my company for a long time to come.

Joan often told me that one day I would have to "step out of the boat" and trust God, referring to when Peter walked on the water to Jesus. She contended the only way to learn trust involved risk.

"Oh, I don't think that will happen to me," I confidently responded. "God knows my temperament. He understands my need for security, to see those paychecks showing up twice a month. He won't ask *me* to step out onto nothing and trust Him."

Wrong! I learned the hard way that when God wants to get our attention or lead us in a new direction, He has a way of making circumstances extremely uncomfortable.

For ten years I had enjoyed serving under a great manager, a man whose ability I respected and who treated me with respect for *my* ability. Much to my disappointment, he was swept away to another area in one of those typical corporate upheavals. My new manager had a picky, authoritarian style. Like a cat poised to pounce on a mouse, she watched and waited for someone to step out of line. I chafed under the tension.

Tearfully, I related my dilemma to Joan.

"I can't start over. What will I do? What kind of job will I get? How can I live on a drastically reduced income? Yet I know this work situation is dragging me down."

"Joy, you can trust God. He won't let you down. If this is the way to go, He will provide and care for you," she gently responded.

"But . . . but . . ." I spluttered.

Joan's response was always the same, "He is trustworthy."

I spent the whole of Labor Day weekend isolated in my condo, agonizing over my decision—I'm a master at agonizing—and searching the scriptures for guidance.

"Please, God, don't let me make a horrible mistake," I begged.

Back to the Hebrews

Once more my mind transported me back to the Sinai. God had provided guidance to Moses and the Israelites. Maybe there was something in the story that would give me direction.

The Living Bible's narrative conveys in earthy, understandable terms what was going on with the Israelites as they camped in the desert. God told Moses to send representatives northward to spy out the land, people, and villages in the territory He had promised them. They were instructed to bring back samples of the crops for the people to see and to not be afraid of what they might find—God would go with them. Moses selected twelve men, two of whom were Joshua, Moses' understudy, and Caleb. The men left and the people waited expectantly for their return.

Forty days later they showed up. A buzz of excitement ran through the camp as they came into view, carrying an abundance of produce. Even from a distance it was obvious the land was indeed fertile. But murmurs rippled through the crowd as the men came near. Joshua and Caleb enthusiastically greeted everyone, glad to be back. The looks on the faces of the other ten, however, conveyed not joy but wide-eyed, conspicuous fear. They agreed the land was lush, but the people occupying it were terrifying. Powerful tribes of unusually tall people lived in walled cities. Any attempt to confront them would be rash and foolhardy. The spies felt like grasshoppers in comparison.

Joshua and Caleb held a different view. Yes, the land was magnificent and lush. Yes, the people were well-armed and physically imposing. But Yahweh, who had brought them to this point, had promised to be with them on the journey. He was well able to help them deal with whatever they would face moving into the new land. The conflicting reports caused enormous consternation and controversy in the camp.

Then all the people began weeping aloud, and they continued through the night. Their words rose in a great chorus of complaint against Moses and Aaron. "We wish we had died in Egypt," they wailed, "or even here in the wilderness, rather than be taken into this country ahead of us. Jehovah will kill us there, and our wives and little ones will become slaves. Let's get out of here and return to Egypt!" The idea swept the camp. "Let's elect a leader to take us back to Egypt!" they shouted.[33]

Moses and Aaron were dismayed at the palpable sense of fear rising in the encampment. Joshua and Caleb continued to plead with the people to be reasonable. They said again: "It is a wonderful country ahead, and the Lord loves us. He will bring us safely into the land and give it to us. It is very fertile, a land 'flowing with milk and honey'! Oh, do not rebel against the Lord, and do not fear the people of the land. For they are but bread for us to eat! The Lord is with us and he has removed his protection from them! Don't be afraid of them!" [34]

The decibel level in the camp rose as arguments broke out and people split into factions. It was crisis time for the Israelites. Finally, a consensus was reached. Obviously their faith and trust in Moses (and Yahweh) was misplaced. Nobody in their right mind would lead a horde of former slaves against powerful warriors. Yahweh had done some amazing things for them in the past, but what guarantee did they have that He would be there for them in the future? Moses had gotten them into this mess; the solution was to stone him. And while they were at it, they would also stone Joshua and Caleb.

Down on the ground, Moses entreated God to do something as the situation spiraled out of control. God's frustration rose to the point where He told Moses He had a new plan. He would wipe these complaining, willful, whining people out of existence and start over again with Moses. Compassionate Moses begged God to reconsider. He presented the human viewpoint by pointing out that Yahweh's reputation could be negatively affected by such action. The nations and tribes, who had observed the adventures of this strange group led by an invisible God, would conclude that their Yahweh was not trustworthy, that He intended all along to lure them into the wilderness to kill them.

God relented and once more forgave the people's rebellion.

But as always, there were consequences to actions. God struck dead the ten spies who induced fear and incited the rebellion. Terrified, the people frantically tried to backpedal. Now that those faithless spies who had negatively influenced their thinking were gone, they wanted to switch sides and follow Caleb and Joshua. In fact, they got up early the next morning, repentant and ready to march forward to the Promised Land. But it was too late.

God then addressed the core issue, rejection of Him and distrust of His care. He vowed to reverse His original plan. The people were certain they would be conquered and their children would become slaves of the warriors occupying the land. God told them He would bring their *children* safely into the Promised Land, while the adults would wander like nomads for the next forty years until they died, one year for each day the spies spent on their journey. Every person twenty years and older who had complained against Him would die in the wilderness, Caleb and Joshua being the only exceptions.

Decision Time

The message of the story came through to me loud and clear. I had the choice to move forward or hang back.

My crab-like nature causes me to zigzag several times before making any progress. I prayed. I agonized. I peered into the future, trying to find a road sign, while my emotions quivered in terror at the prospect of leaving the security of Delta.

One line in my inspirational desk calendar leapt off the page: "You have to keep growing, or you start dying." Those few words summed up my state of mind and heart—I was dying on the inside.

Something deep inside urged me to take a chance. Could I step out in faith as my grandparents and parents had done? I reflected on Grandma Connie's writings and the many instances where God honored her trust in Him to provide. I had enough illustrations to know God answered the fervent prayers of His children. Would He answer mine? But blind trust was more than I could muster, so I came up with a brilliant solution to the dilemma, the concept of which had been bred into me from my earliest days.

Here's a Good Plan, Lord!

The bent toward literal interpretation of scripture and the definition of "faith" passed down from my grandparents was deeply embedded. I read selectively, picked out and focused on all the good promises. My "get from God" mentality was finely tuned. I conveniently ignored anything dealing with hardship.

According to the Bible, Jesus said I could ask anything in His name and it would be given to me.[35] I decided to put this to the test, constructing a very reasonable argument as the basis for my request.

I wanted to be involved in some aspect of missions, but so many mission organizations were clamoring for funds. I didn't want to *take* from missions, I wanted to *give*. If God would send me a huge amount of money, I could devote my energies to administering the fund, supporting mission activities around the world, and of course, I would be well able to take care of myself financially. I didn't have any rich relatives or benefactors, so I asked to win the Reader's Digest Sweepstakes. I'd been a long-time customer, and surely now would be a good time to win the grand prize. There was no doubt in my mind that a sovereign God was able to do this. I even found a scripture to support my position: "The lot is cast into the lap, but its every decision is from the LORD."[36] I presented this win-win plan in prayer and asked Jesus to bring it to fulfillment. This would enable me to sail into my retirement years with no financial worries, free to devote myself to God's work.

Taking a deep breath, I said, "Here I come, God. Don't let me crash" and signed up for early retirement. I wrote on the back of one of my business cards, "The rest of my life, the *best* of my life" and stuck it on my dresser mirror. If all went according to plan, *my* plan, I wouldn't be in poverty long—just until the sweepstakes money came through.

I am embarrassed now to reveal my immature reasoning. Fortunately, God's patience is limitless. I was profoundly sincere but so misguided. Yet my response was merely an updated version of the thinking of the Israelites whose preconceived ideas kept getting tangled in their efforts to get to know the God who led them. They thrashed around, latching onto anything that would spare them from having to practice raw trust in an invisible God.

One Day at a Time

No sooner had I made the decision to take early retirement than I began worrying about being away from the structure and social contacts of work. I knew I had to take several months off to recuperate physically and mentally, but this raised the specter of too much time alone. It would be awful if I took this giant step out of my security zone and then landed myself in the ditch of depression. Again, I strained to see into the future, to have it all planned out in advance. And again, I anticipated the worst.

"Joy, stop worrying about January when it's only November," Joan chided. "Worry about January in January!"

So on December 31, 1992, I walked out of the gates of Delta Air Lines and took my first tentative steps into the windswept desert with God. I drew strength from Karle Wilson Baker's words, "Courage is fear that has said its prayers."

POINTER: Seeking After God Always Involves Risk

- It's unfortunate, but true. God's first test of our sincerity calls for us to leave our comfort zone. Adventures don't happen in sheltered coves.

- Have you felt a "tug" to venture into something unknown, to take action which appears foolhardy according to conventional wisdom?

- What do you feel you're being called to do?

- A good test is to determine if this is an emotional reaction or if it remains in your heart and mind.

- If it sticks, pay attention!

POINTER REFLECTIONS:

15

SOLITUDE AND SILENCE

He restores my soul.

Psalm 23:3 (NASB)

To my amazement, I didn't fall into the ditch of depression. I reveled in having hours to myself. What then seemed merely a time to rest and get organized turned out to be the beginning of my long, slow healing process.

My condo had a delightful sunroom with windows on three sides looking out onto beautiful, tall trees. This became my therapy room as I spent countless hours watching the pine needles grow. It was a treat to be off my past rigid schedule, free to putter through each day. I worked my way through a pile of mystery stories. Long postponed chores got done, including putting hundreds of pictures in albums. I spent hours looking at scenes from the past—people, events, places.

Silence is a lost quality in our modern world. It's almost impossible to be anywhere without experiencing the intrusion of noise. CNN blares at me from airport monitors. Marketers have convinced merchants that loud pop music is as necessary to shopping as the merchandise itself. Even churches, the last bastion of hope for quiet meditation, offer little or no opportunity for silence. Noise has become a way of stifling the voices we don't want to hear.

Filling the emptiness around me worked well for many years. The moments were rare when the car radio, tape player, or television fell silent. But now I craved uninterrupted quiet. My troubled soul sought solace in silence, in its healing, restoring balm. The prophet Hosea offered an interesting perspective on God's purpose in leading us away from the crowds and activities of life. "Therefore I am now going to allure her; I will lead her into the wilderness and speak tenderly to her. There I will give her back her vineyards, and will make the Valley of Achor a door of hope." (Achor means "trouble.")[37]

Soul Nourishment

I always felt chastened when I heard people announce that they had read the Bible through, often several times. A block in my thinking turned what I believed to be a beneficial venture into a mind-numbing chore. A compilation of scriptures, *Daily Light on the Daily Path,* offered an appealing compromise. The morning and evening segments covered a theme. I liked the fact the book contained nothing but scripture verses—no commentaries, no study notes, no interpretation, nobody's thoughts. I sensed that if I were going to learn about God, I had to block out the clamoring voices of others.

I made myself focus on less appealing scriptures, those that gave insight into the purpose behind suffering and difficulties. Time and again I ran across the words "unfailing love" as an expression of God's emotion toward His creatures. Each time I read the words it had the effect of warm sunshine on a block of ice. "Unfailing love" formed a building block in my understanding as I continued to discover the character of the ethereal, transcendent God.

Oh, No, It's Boot Camp!

One evening a documentary on the U.S. Navy SEALS had me riveted to the television. I watched the team endure the ultimate boot camp experience—immersion in freezing water for hours, interminable periods of slithering through mud, four hours sleep in five days and nights, survival tests almost beyond physical limits. Some dropped out through exhaustion, but those who withstood the tortures were honored with the prestigious designation of "Navy SEAL." They were fit, they were trained, and they were ready to perform whatever role was needed for their country. What commitment! What dedication!

To my dismay, instead of God performing the instant, transforming miracle I wanted, He recruited me into Boot Camp. To my further dismay, I learned this training didn't begin with heroically leaping out of a helicopter over a churning sea. It started with push-ups—thousands of them!

The Apostle Paul accurately identified the area of weakness where my "push-ups" needed to begin:

Do not be conformed to this world—this age, fashioned after and adapted to its external, superficial customs. But be transformed (changed) by the [entire] renewal of your mind—by its new ideals and its new attitude—so that you may prove [for yourselves] what is the good and acceptable and perfect will of God, even the thing which is good and acceptable and perfect [in His sight for you].[38]

One day, as I listened to *The Hour of Power* on television, Robert H. Schuller introduced a book by Martin Seligman, *Learned Optimism*. I realized with a shock that I, who had been grounded in the hopefulness of "faith," was a negative thinker. I had a decided tendency to allow my thoughts to slide downhill into doom.

I bought the book and feverishly began reading, searching for anything tangible to help structure my wayward thoughts. Unlike my perpetually optimistic father, I have a melancholy temperament. While I doubted I would ever become a sunny optimist, perhaps I could achieve some sort of middle ground.

Using my newfound insight, I began the hard work of reprogramming the computer of my thinking. In addition to scripture, I gathered positive messages, clippings from magazines, posters to hang in my closet where I viewed them daily, anything that offered helpful input. I sent away for Dr. Schuller's desk calendar, *Putting Your Faith Into Action Today!*[39] It offered 365 daily devotions for positive living.

One scripture became a lifeline, a source of encouragement to keep going: "I would have despaired unless I had believed that I would see the goodness of the LORD *in the land of the living*" (italics mine).[40] I had to believe in the possibility of hope and healing while still alive, that one didn't simply endure the pain and hardship until it was all wiped away in heaven. I set my will to turn my negative viewpoint around.

Gradually new data was programmed into the hard drive of my memory. I found as I put my mind in random search mode that the scriptures had a way of popping up at precisely the right moment to give me the insight or direction I needed.

Little did I know how desperately I would cling to those scriptures in the coming days.

POINTER: Reprogramming Thinking is Work!

- Consider areas of your thinking that may need changing.

- Begin to gather materials that will help you, books, magazine articles, posters, anything that grabs your attention and "speaks" to you.

- Place these where you can see them every day.

POINTER REFLECTIONS:

16

LEARNING TO TRUST AN INVISIBLE GOD IS HARD

I will instruct you (says the Lord) and guide you along the best pathway for your life; I will advise you and watch your progress.

Psalm 32:8 (TLB)

Anticipation mounted as the time of the Reader's Digest Sweepstakes drawing arrived. I went on high alert for the sound of the telephone, hovered at the mailbox, and listened with half an ear for the doorbell to announce a special delivery letter. While planning the many commendable directions in which I would spread my largesse, I also pictured myself in a hot new sports car or reclining on a chaise lounge on a luxury cruise, dressed in stylish, fine quality clothes.

Days passed and nothing happened. The awful truth drenched my soaring spirits, landing me with a thud back in reality. I had "exercised faith" as best I knew how, and it hadn't worked. Was "acting in faith" and getting a positive response from God confined only to those who were in ministry? Perhaps I didn't deserve anything so good?

I floundered, exploring job options, weighing my recognized skills against my limited education (by American standards) and lack of credentials. Despite my confusion, I still had the strong desire to invest myself in something that had eternal significance. The answer surfaced: go to work for a ministry.

I learned that an organization relocating two miles from my home needed someone to set up their office. The pay was abysmal, but it was a job with a ministry. Surely this was the Lord's leading?

What a disaster! My boss had a severe case of verbal diarrhea. I am convinced his recorder was permanently attached to his hand. Hour after hour I sat at the computer transcribing dictation. I hated putting someone else's words on paper after having spent so many years creating my own letters. Surely I didn't give up my well-paying, prestigious job at Delta for this, earning less than half the money? Maybe I had misheard, misunderstood, or taken matters into my own hands—stepped out of the "will of God"—and now I was in this mess on my own.

Being forced to learn new technology turned into a small plus. When "the cat" was out of the office, this "mouse" played—with a mouse! I sat by myself in utter misery and learned Windows™.

The Reader's Digest Sweepstakes incident had been an embarrassing fiasco, although I did manage to keep private how much I counted on winning. The Deceiver had a grand time, pointing out that my fervent prayers for financial security had failed. God had not led me into a bright, new world of opportunity and service. I was in this on my own. I needed to take charge of my life and make the best of my circumstances. God was up there, but He was distant and uninvolved. Circumstances became more difficult as I grappled with relational and professional conflicts and continued on my unappealing path of frugality in light of my diminished income. The crossbar of my will teetered dangerously.

I had set out to prove to myself what Christianity was about and to see if it were possible to have a one-on-one relationship with God. What I encountered were glimpses of truth behind a veil of inexplicable circumstances. Christianity did not work the way I thought it did. God did not work the way I thought He should. Nevertheless, as I retraced my path, there were times when I had no explanation for how situations turned out other than that God had overruled, overshadowed, and acted on my behalf. I could not say I had a relationship with Him, yet honesty would not let me deny that I had an awareness of His presence.

This Is Not What I Signed Up For

Sometime during my formative years I developed the notion that when I chose to become a Christian and set my will to learn about God and His ways I was embarking on a journey comparable to a luxury cruise. I was shocked to discover that I had instead signed up for the army. It was Private Benjamin all over again! I wanted to be a pampered, privileged passenger and found myself a lowly, miserable grunt in the trenches.

I thought again of the U.S. Navy SEALS. *Their* determination held fast; mine ran the risk of crumbling. Flipping through the Bible, I read:

> Though the fig tree does not bud and there are no grapes on the vines, though the olive crop fails and the fields produce no food, though there are no sheep in the pen and no cattle in the stalls, yet I will rejoice in the Lord, I will be joyful in God my Savior.[41]

This was a sad state of affairs. I had to concede my situation wasn't nearly as bad as that described by the prophet Habakkuk. The words "yet I will rejoice in the Lord" pierced through my self-pity. God had not abandoned me. Life was uncertain right now, but I was still the beneficiary of His amazing grace.

This struggle centered on my will. In my mind, I could accept being in the army; however, I at least wanted to be a general. Instead, my duties called for unquestioning obedience and implicit trust in my Commander-in-Chief. The next verse revealed the purpose in my starting out in the trenches:

> The Sovereign Lord is my strength; he makes my feet like the feet of a deer, he enables me to tread on the heights.

A wise God wanted to teach me how to negotiate my way through the hills and valleys of life with the sure-footedness and confidence of a deer bounding across craggy mountain slopes. The deer that live above the tree line exist on lichen and undergrowth, not hay and fine Kentucky blue grass. My mind focused only on God's gifts, or lack of them. I needed to turn my negative viewpoint around, to switch my attention to the Giver instead.

God, Please *Do* Something!

Patience has never been one of my strong traits. I am by nature a planner, and planners live in the future, anticipating every eventuality, good and bad. Waiting powerlessly is excruciating. In the middle of a sweltering summer, I long for the cooler days of late September. Then when February rolls around and tantalizes me with a few warmer days, I can't wait for spring.

What strikes me about the seasons is their implacability to my wants and wishes. I can throw a tantrum and demand that spring arrive. I can defy nature and put my tender plants in early. But spring will come when it is ready. The seasons change according to God's timetable, not mine. Fussing and fuming alters nothing.

I recalled bygone days when I complained to Dad about what I thought were unwarranted waiting periods, when I had urgent needs and nothing happened to ease the situation. His wise reply stuck with me.

"When God is silent, He is not inactive, inattentive, uninvolved, or uncaring. Think of this time as a 'rest' in a music score. There is total silence while the conductor beats out the tempo with his baton. At the appropriate moment, all instruments are raised, the conductor gives the nod, and the music begins again in perfect harmony. The magnificence of the piece is enhanced by the 'rest,' the interlude that preceded it."

The Bible records many "rests" in God's timetable. Probably the most significant of these was the approximately 400 years between the ending of the Old Testament and the beginning of the New Testament. Talk about silence! From the perspective of the Jews who were waiting anxiously for Messiah to arrive, it seemed they had been abandoned by God. They heard nothing from Him—no prophet spoke His words, no visions gave assurance that He was paying attention.

Yet history reveals that God was working behind the scenes, preparing the world stage for the arrival of Jesus and the introduction of a new Kingdom. Wars were fought, empires established, leaders positioned, and the hearts of people were prepared for the message that Jesus would bring. Eventually, the Romans conquered the known world. To rule effectively, they built roads to the farthest regions of the empire. The Greeks introduced a common language. The Jews patiently and hopefully waited for Messiah. Then when everything was prepared and in place, Jesus was born. Later the gospel was spread through the Greek language, transported along Roman roads, by Jews whose patient hope had been rewarded.

Remembering this had a steadying influence, although I fervently hoped God wouldn't take 400 years with my situation! I read somewhere that it is better to live with a void in your life than fill it with an inferior presence. This sounds noble and wise, but it takes every ounce of determination and trust in an invisible God to accomplish it. I clung desperately to the hope that God was, indeed, paying attention and had not abandoned me.

God IS Aware!

Fall came early to Atlanta that year. As I opened my front door, the coolness from outside crept inside. Turning the heat on didn't help much. As I pulled my winter robe from its summer hiding spot, I remembered how uncomfortable it was. It had served me well for twenty years, but it had unfortunately not grown with me. The mirror confirmed my suspicion it belonged to my little sister. In my affluent Delta days, I would have gleefully headed to the mall, whipped out a credit card, and returned with the latest and greatest in robes. But times had changed, and I had to prioritize my spending. I needed a new winter robe, and the bank balance said, "No way!"

If Dad had been alive, I could have put a winter robe on my Christmas list, and he would have gladly given it to me—or provided the money. I stood staring at the figure in the worn, ill-fitting robe while tears filled my eyes. No Dad, no Mom, a sister far away. No husband or children to give me Christmas presents. I was alone. It was pitiful!

Then the Spirit gently spoke to my mind, reminding me this wasn't true. Jesus promised never to forsake me. His tender words assured me my Heavenly Father knew my needs.[42] Warmth unrelated to my skimpy robe permeated my being. So what if my robe was old and uncomfortable, at least I had one.

A few weeks later, Macy's department store mailed one of their former best customers a notice about Customer Appreciation Day. If I visited the store by a certain day, I could fill out an entry for one of their grand prizes. The first and second prizes were vacations in Mexico and Hawaii, places I had already visited, so these weren't of much interest. Besides, they would involve spending money. The third caught my attention—a $1,000 shopping spree! *That certainly would be nice, Lord,* I thought. Despite my near poverty status, I decided it would be worth a visit to the store. After all, I needed pantyhose.

I made my huge pantyhose purchase and wandered aimlessly for a while. Almost out the door on the way home, I remembered the sweepstakes entry still in my purse. By now my feet were sore, I was downstairs, and the entry box was upstairs. I debated making the effort, but something urged me to go up the escalator and turn in my entry.

Ten days later, I picked up my mail and saw a letter addressed to me from Macy's. My eyes bulged as I read that I was the lucky winner of the $1,000 Shopping Spree! I didn't know whether to laugh or cry, so I did both. It was as though Jesus hugged me and said, "See, Joy, your earthly father is not the only one who can give you good gifts."

On December 4 I spent four glorious hours being escorted around the department store by one of Macy's managers. Needless to say, the first item I selected was a lovely, warm, long, roomy, wrap-around robe. I drifted through one department after another, indulging myself in new clothes, home furnishings, jewelry, makeup, and shoes, while the manager kept a running tally of my spending. I ended up with a positive balance of $2.73, which I graciously let Macy's keep.

Why didn't I win the Reader's Digest Sweepstakes, yet now won this Macy's prize? They both involved random selection. Years later, I realized the first related to my expectation of God's approval of *my* plans. Even more significant was the recognition that He had an infinitely better plan in mind. The second was the spontaneous response of a loving God to someone who desperately needed an encouraging hug. God may be invisible, but He was aware, and He cared. He was also incredibly creative.

A Temporary Reprieve

A former boss at Delta Air Lines rescued me from my dreaded job at the ministry by offering me contract work at a good salary. I happily accepted.

Unfortunately, my CPA and I had a major miscommunication during that first year of retirement. When I submitted my tax information, I learned to my horror that I owed over $1,500 to Uncle Sam! Not only did I have to come up with the money by April 15, but I also had to increase my deductions from my already meager pension.

Doubt plagued my mind. The Deceiver had a grand time.

"Well, Joy, your fervent prayer for financial security hasn't been answered, has it? Obviously you misread the situation in leaving Delta. Why not face up to it—you're on your own. Take charge of your life and learn to make the best of things."

My previously comfortable, ordered existence had become like a roller coaster ride. A devotional reading steered my straying thoughts back to my scale concept. Trust starts as an act of will. Feelings are totally unreliable. The solution to my dilemma lay in the power of my will. I could give it all up, or I could set my mind determinedly against doubt and see where the road led.

Thinking I might find some clue as to what was going on, I turned back to the Hebrews' story to see what I could learn from their experience.

The God Who Plans Ahead

The lesson this time centered on the anticipatory providence of God. I loved the assurance given in the Book of Numbers, "The ark of the covenant of the LORD went before them during those three days to find them a place to rest."[43] God took the trouble to seek out the next resting place before leading His people forward.

God doesn't slap His forehead and say, "Oops! Forgot about Joy!" He anticipates. He plans. He provides. I could see that God had foreseen my tax mistake and had gone before me to provide a way to meet my need.

My contract work ended, and I was again faced with "Now what?" The unhappy experience working at the ministry left me at a loss to know which way to go. I had a graduate degree from the University of Life, but no real academic credentials to present to a prospective employer.

When my windfall didn't materialize, I realized I had better find a full-time job. Despite my disappointment over my train-wrecked plans, I anticipated that

God would graciously give me an easy transition into a new career. The reality was far different. I encountered numerous obstacles, and my future looked as bleak as windswept sand dunes. I found it decidedly uncomfortable living in the "desert" and following the leading of an invisible God.

Whining Time

Time and again I read that whenever things didn't go the way the Hebrews wanted, they complained and whined. Transferring God's past goodness into the present and projecting it into the future became a gigantic challenge, resulting in repeated failure.

They needed water; God provided water. They needed food; God provided manna. Then they got tired of the sameness of the manna and craved meat. Numbers tells us, "The rabble with them began to crave other food, and again the Israelites started wailing and said, 'If only we had meat to eat! We remember the fish we ate in Egypt at no cost—also the cucumbers, melons, leeks, onions, and garlic. But now we have lost our appetite; we never see anything but this manna!'"[44]

The people squelched memories of the harshness of the Egyptian taskmasters and the grueling grind of slavery. All they chose to recall was the availability of delectable food.

Human nature hadn't changed over the centuries, and I was no different. When faced with difficult circumstances, I looked back and remembered selectively. I had been given a taste of freedom. God was slowly but surely proving His faithfulness and trustworthiness. Did

I really wish I were back at Delta? The truthful answer was a resounding "no."

Help!

"Lord, help! If I don't get a job by the end of August, I won't be able to pay my bills in September," I cried.

My anxiety level rose like a hot air balloon, propelled by the churning in my stomach. But this time, instead of wallowing in confusion and fear, I steadfastly held my will in place. I clung to my support column, seeking guidance and provision. My fumbling efforts to be obedient and follow God's direction had got me into this predicament—I expected Him to mercifully get me out of it.

That didn't stop me from calling Joan to whine about my finances and the future. She listened patiently and then calmly said, "Joy, do you need it now? Do you have money for today?"

"Well, yes," I admitted.

"Then don't worry today about what will happen in the future. When you need it, it will be there. God is trustworthy. He won't let you down."

Joan once more tapped into my airline background, asking me to picture the pilot of a small plane. It is night, the weather is deteriorating and fuel is running dangerously low. The landing strip is completely hidden in the darkness. The pilot strains forward, peering into the blackness. Where are those landing lights? If they don't come on soon, a crash is inevitable. The plane rocks in the wind as he struggles to keep course and balance. Anxiety rises. He can do nothing but trust that the people below are alert and will turn on the landing lights in time. The ground looms closer, and still there is no break in the blackness. Suddenly, two rows of lights appear just ahead. With overwhelming relief, the pilot turns the aircraft and centers his approach. With a thud and a bounce, the plane lands and comes to a stop. He is safe.

On August 26 my "landing lights" came on. I got a job on staff at the church I attended. That afternoon there was a message on my recorder, "Well, He rescued you one inch off the concrete, didn't He?"

Joan had proved her point.

POINTER: Review Past Experiences

- Have you experienced instances of unexplained provision or amazingly coincidental timing?

- Could these have been God's intervention, His love reaching out toward you?

- Do you sense an overshadowing, caring Presence even though circumstances may be confusing or difficult?

- Battles of will are inevitable. In such times, place a list of God's attributes where you can read them frequently.

POINTER REFLECTIONS:

17

THE CHURCH: CONDUIT OR OBSTACLE?

Thou art the Christ, the Son of the living God.
                                Matthew 16:16 (TNIV)

. . . upon this rock I will build My church.
                                Matthew 16:18 (TNIV)

Once more I started out optimistically on my path of trying to blend my skills with the needs of a ministry. During the interview process for the church job I made sure my future boss didn't have a dictation recorder as an extension of his hand. He assured me he did not.

I considered it an honor to serve on the staff of this large, prestigious church, with its expanding television ministry. I had undoubtedly found my post-Delta niche, was in the center of God's will, and could stay until my final retirement.

The Director of Administration and I worked well together. He goes down in my memory as one of the nicest managers of my long working career— kind, fair, honest, straightforward, supportive. He showed appreciation for my mind, encouraged my abilities, and treated me, as a woman, with unfailing respect.

Within a year, however, questions related to "the church" threw me into a quandary. Devotion to the church had been drilled into me, and I faithfully attended despite my questionings. I remained convinced my road to inner peace had to center on serving God through the church.

Although I believed my route to God had been cleared in my mind, in actuality, my path to the invisible God was as effectively blocked as the Israelites' with their need for visible Egyptian gods. Without realizing it, I had developed a hierarchy in my pathway thinking:

Step by step the obstacles between God and me had been cleared. Mom and Dad were gone. I now found myself facing a major hurdle—the church. A wise God knew the underlying issues that needed to surface and be resolved, and had engineered my circumstances.

Factions, Squabbling, Showdown!

The telephone at my desk rang for what seemed like the hundredth time that day. I took a deep breath and picked up the receiver. It was yet another upset member of the congregation. I listened courteously, then hung up, hoping for a few moments respite from the on-slaught. This was unreal! "Church wars" was definitely not what I had in mind when years ago I told the Lord I wanted to be involved in something that had eternal significance.

I had been aware for some time of undercurrents among the leadership. A power struggle seethed beneath the spiritual exterior presented to the world, couched in the context of "adhering to scriptural guidelines and instruction." What it boiled down to was a monstrous fight based on interpretation of scripture regarding the qualifications of a pastor to lead a congregation.

I found myself in the hot seat listening to members, nonmembers, and sundry parties expressing their opin-ions on the controversy surrounding the pastor's mari-tal problems. Opposing factions held equally dogmatic views on the subject. The fight was fierce and brutal. Unity was shattered. Many people were confused and hurting. Others became rampant militants, expound-ing their views with the conviction of politicians on the campaign trail. The fact that this was not a clear-cut issue related to sexual misconduct, embezzlcment, or blatant heresy added to the divisiveness.

Instead of being launched into a rewarding, fruit-ful phase of my life, I had landed in a hornet's nest. Resentment, mixed with bewilderment, simmered in me. Had I misread God's leading in taking this job? It had seemed so providential. Every part of me screamed "Get out!" But I had a wonderful boss who needed my support, and I needed the money—a great deterrent for rash moves.

A showdown loomed. The tension drained my spiritual, physical, and emotional reserves. Worse yet, the conflict uncapped an emotional geyser.

Every day my disillusionment with the church grew. Each telephone call resonated with the controversies that had drifted around the edges of my environment all my life. Dad had faced hostility within the church organization's hierarchy; Mom had suffered criticism from our local congregation. Pools of theological interpretation had swirled around me as individuals vied for acceptance of their particular teaching. Dad's congregation loved him, but the pews were filled with humans, people with weaknesses often compounded when placed in the context of the battle between spirituality and "the flesh"—an individual's humanness.

I forced the cap back on the geyser and endeavored to regain my emotional balance. When reconciliation was no longer an option, the church split down the middle.

A Power Struggle

I wish I could say that calm returned, the remnant picked up the pieces, and we all went on "doing the Lord's work." Regrettably, another layer of seething undercurrent surfaced. This time the power struggle was internal. My boss and I were harshly criticized for our corporate image. We both had backgrounds in the business world and were endeavoring to apply our expertise in efficiently running our area while balancing integrity and loyalty to leadership. He resigned, and that same day I learned of another job opportunity and turned in my resignation.

My disillusionment and disgust with "the church" and the behavior of so-called Christians overflowed. Instead of the care of my soul, which I thought was the reason for a church's existence, all I had gotten my entire life was criticism—as a child, and now as an adult. Additionally, no longer could I trust the church leadership, those in whom I had placed confidence. How could I rely on what was being stated from the pulpit when there was such a disparity between words and actions?

I resigned from membership and vowed never again to join a church. *If this is what the church represents, I don't want any part of it.* Yet in my calmer moments I craved spiritual solace.

Putting It In Perspective

A good friend sympathetic to my battered soul invited me to Atlanta's Peachtree Presbyterian Church. An air of calm enveloped me as I entered the beautiful sanctuary, like someone putting soothing ointment on a burning wound. Sunlight streamed through tall windows; there was an atmosphere of reverence as the pews quietly filled. The words of the old hymns reminded me of the enduring message of the Christian faith.

God did His amazing thing again, speaking to me at precisely the time I needed to hear from Him. The sermon topic on this particular Sunday was "The Church." The speaker made a statement that blew open a window in my understanding. He told us it was okay to feel ambivalent about the church. On the one hand we are drawn to it for all the good done and for what the church symbolizes—the body of believers. On the other hand, we are repelled because of the bad associated with it, historically and in our present culture. Then, like someone turning a kaleidoscope, he put it all in perspective by emphasizing that the organized church is still God's primary instrument of ministry in the world. It is designed to minister to the ungodly, the needy, the hurting inside and outside its walls, to the true disciples of Christ in the congregation, and those who might attend for dubious reasons. God uses the church to reach out to others.

During the week, I seemed to hear Jesus say, "Joy, it's okay to feel ambivalent about the church. I feel the same way sometimes!" A load lifted off my shoulders.

Two Levels of "Church"

For the first time I realized how God and the church were intertwined in my mind. Devotion to God through "the church" had become an essential part of my identity. After all, this had been instilled in me from my highchair days. I absorbed the idea the church was my way to God, the way to gaining His acceptance, receiving His love, and enjoying His blessings. Attending church, being involved in church—this is what Christians did. So for all the years I lived in Durban, I served in some capacity. The lurking suspicion that I would be rejected by God, my parents, my extended family, and the congregation kept me going. I gave to the church, of myself and of my finances. I sought to uphold the teachings of the church. I tried to be a good representative of the church, and of Mom and Dad's ministry.

Yet through all those years of striving, I did not sense the church had ministered to me. In my estimation, it had robbed me. My view of "the church" colored my view of God. I equated my ambiguous interactions with "the church" with my interaction with God and vice versa.

Looking at the equal-arm balance model, I wondered: Where does the church belong? On the support column that represents God or in the suspended pan of *Others?*

My mind flashed back to a return visit to Durban. Reports had filtered across the ocean on progress in Dad's former church. As often happens when there is a change in ministry, people drift away, some to other churches or denominations, some to other parts of the country. In fact, there had been quite a turnover in the congregation. I sat in the sanctuary and speculated where all the familiar faces might be. Had they wandered away from God?

Over the next few weeks, I had opportunity to meet up with many of these former members. And I had a blinding revelation. These people had left the local church, but the "church" established in their hearts was as vibrant as ever.

I realized there are two levels of meaning for the word "church." One is the "church universal," a spiritual entity, created by God and introduced by Jesus, comprised of all the people who accepted the basic tenets of the Christian faith as expressed in The Apostles' Creed.

It crossed denominational, cultural, and geographic boundaries. This church, the Kingdom of God in the hearts of individuals, had survived over 2,000 years and would continue to survive despite adversity and persecution. It would not be overpowered by Satan's efforts to undermine it, dilute its effectiveness, or cause confusion and dissension in its ranks.

The other is the organized or denominational church, the one to which people go on Sundays to worship or Saturdays to get married. This "church" can range through the elaborate cathedrals of Europe, steepled churches on Main Street, converted warehouses, school buildings, or thatch-covered structures in some primitive setting. The purpose is to gather for communal worship, Biblical instruction, and the fellowship of like minds and hearts.

By an act of my will and in response to the Spirit's call, I had joined the Church of Jesus Christ, committing to be His follower. This was my vertical, spiritual connection. The "church universal" belongs in the vertical support column. It is inextricably linked and intertwined with the Triune God. As Jesus said to the disciples, "In that day you shall know that I am in My Father, and you in Me, and I in you."[45]

The local, organized church is a horizontal connection and therefore belongs in the pan of *Others*. It plays a significant role, but is secondary to my personal relationship with the God who designed me to live free in fellowship with Him. This "church" falls into the category of "loving my neighbor."

The Crux of My Confusion

A vague thought drifted around in my mind, like a dangling spider searching for some place to attach itself. Had I uncovered the crux of where my understanding of Christianity broke down, where in fact it always broke down and had done for centuries—human interpretation?

Up to this point, I tracked with my grandparents and parents in my beliefs in God, Jesus, and the Spirit, although the latter remained confusing. But now I had moved beyond the essentials of the faith to individual interpretation and application. And this is where it became murky.

I floundered, unsure of what I could legitimately ask God for. I acknowledged His good track record in taking care of my material needs—never too much, but always enough, and always timely. But beyond that I was uncertain. Then I came across a prayer I felt generic and broad enough to allow God plenty of room to act while I kept my hands off the controls, "Remember me with favor, my God."[46]

Oswald Chambers articulated my struggle. "The real trial of faith is not that we find it difficult to trust God, but that God's character has to be cleared in our own minds." This could mean long spells of excruciating isolation. Chambers warned that we should never confuse the trial of faith with the ordinary discipline of life. Many times what we called the trial of faith was the inevitable result of being alive. "Faith in the Bible is faith in God against everything that contradicts Him—I will remain true to God's character whatever He may do. [...] Faith is unutterable trust in God, trust which never dreams that He will not stand by us."[*]

God hadn't done what I wanted Him to do. However much sugar-coating I put on it, I had called the shots, dreaming up plans and expecting God to not only endorse them but pour out indescribable blessings as well. I realized how the fuzziness of the role of human will had distorted my picture of God's way, how all those stories of my grandparents and parents had lodged in my mind and formed my own interpretation of how God worked. Then when my preconceived ideas fell apart, it left me floundering.

I decided I should begin looking at what God said He *would* do based on who He was, not at what I expected Him to do. Summoning my shaky will, I renewed my commitment.

The Bible said God was merciful—therefore He would be compassionate toward my failings and misguided thinking.

The Bible said God was generous—even when He withheld His bounty from me.

The Bible said God was faithful—He did not act capriciously.

The Bible said God was kind—He was not in the business of arranging circumstances to torture me.

The Bible said God was just—He acted impartially.

The Bible said God was wise—therefore I could assume He would do what He knew to be good for me, whether or not I agreed.

The Bible said God was truthful—He did not lie or change his mind.

The Bible said God was loving—He wanted to bring out the best in me, and in turn give me His best.

God was "there," He was aware, and He cared.

POINTER: Consider the "Two Churches" Concept

- Have you found "the church" to be a conduit to God or an obstacle?

- Does the "two churches" concept help to clear your own path to a relationship with the invisible God? The one church is an invisible, spiritual connection; the other a visible, earthly connection.

There will be periods when God seems deaf, or even unkind. During these times, it is crucial to hold your will in place and trust in His character. Don't allow your mind to dwell on His seeming lack of involvement.

POINTER REFLECTIONS:

PART SIX

THE SUSPENDED PAN OF *OTHERS*

18
WISDOM SCHOOL

You shall love your neighbor as yourself.
Matthew 22:39 (NASB)

Which came first, the chicken or the egg? This age-old question summarized my dilemma as I moved toward examining the pans of *Others* and *Self* suspended from the equal-arm balance's crossbar.

My relationships are a mirror of who I am; I am shaped by my relationships. I react to the attitudes and behavior of others, yet the attitudes and behavior of others already imprinted on me frequently trigger an automatic response.

The turmoil of recent months proved I needed instruction on handling interpersonal conflict. I wanted to develop skill in this area—without looking too deeply at my role in the dispute. My protective instincts told me it would be less conflicting to look at *Others* than at *Self*.

Looking at My Neighbor

The definition of "joy" had been an easy lesson to learn, given my name:

J	=	Jesus First
O	=	Others Second
Y	=	Yourself Last

I had no difficulty grasping the idea of "loving my neighbor," since life in our ministerial household centered on *Others*. Hundreds of people called upon Dad at any time of the day or night, and he promptly responded to their cries for prayer, visitation, or comfort. Mom spent her energies supporting Dad's ministry efforts, running the musical program of the church and exercising her administrative and organizational skills for the benefit of the congregation.

Further, my multicultural environment underscored the awareness of *Others*. We limped along on Dad's meager paycheck from month to month, yet the ten percent tithe came off the top, followed by a mission offering for those less fortunate. I adopted the same pattern when I began earning. My desire to be involved in missions evolved from this early recognition of the needs of *Others*.

While I had an acute awareness of *Others*, I recognized my tendency to remain detached, in all likelihood motivated by self-protection. Circumstances were about to expose me to crucial, yet unexplored, aspects of "my neighbor."

Wisdom School

My daily devotional reading turned my attention to the wisdom literature in the Old Testament: the books of Job, Proverbs, and Ecclesiastes, as well as the Psalms. Hebrew wisdom literature, as distinguished from the wisdom writings of other cultures, was centered on God: "The fear of the Lord is the beginning of knowledge; fools despise wisdom and instruction."[47] In contrast, Egyptian wisdom focused on the wisdom of the sages and on disciplining oneself to accept the trials of life.

I had based my understanding of "wisdom" on Webster's English definition, being the power of judging rightly and following the soundest course of action based on knowledge, experience. But the ancient literature introduced a broader meaning. The Hebrew word *hokmah* (wisdom) was translated "skill for living" because the Jews regarded wisdom in practical terms, a guide for moral behavior and everyday living. *Hokmah* encompassed ethical and spiritual wisdom, wisdom as skill and intelligence, and wisdom as shrewdness.[48]

Skill for living—did I ever need that!

I knew from my piano-playing days that skill was not some mystical quality infused into my mind while I slept. It came from dedication and experience. Concert musicians practiced six to eight hours a day; athletes trained under the most demanding conditions. Acquiring skill in a particular area called for determined effort and a commitment to overcoming obstacles in pursuit of the goal. Proverbs 2 told me to seek after wisdom, and the qualities of discernment, understanding, righteousness, justice, honesty, knowledge, and discretion would blend to produce skill in living.

I adopted a new prayer:

> May I receive the words of wisdom and treasure her commands within me, turning my ear to wisdom and applying my heart to understanding.
>
> If I cry for discernment and lift up my voice for understanding, if I seek her as silver and search for her as for hidden treasures, then I will understand the fear of the Lord and find the knowledge of God. Then I will understand righteousness and justice and honesty—every good path.
>
> For wisdom will enter my heart, and knowledge will be pleasant to my soul. Discretion will protect me, and understanding will guard me.*

Without being aware of it, I found myself enrolled in Wisdom School. The first course in learning to deal with *Others* was "Theological Interpretation 101."

Whose Truth Is True?

My job at the church offered a most appealing perk—a delicious three-course meal served each day.

---

*Kenneth Boa, *Handbook to Prayer*, Atlanta, GA: Trinity House Publishers, Inc. 1993, p. 170. Used by permission.

The leadership's incentive in providing this was not to save me from cooking at home, but to afford staff members opportunities for lunchtime interaction.

I found the mealtime conversations fascinating, different from those in the secular world in that religious views were openly shared. However, nagging questions soon surfaced. I had remained on the periphery of the congregation for many years, content to worship and absorb scriptural instruction on Sundays. Becoming a staff member moved me closer to the heartbeat of the ministry, and teachings and attitudes not apparent from the pulpit emerged.

I was astounded to learn the church did not endorse women teaching men in Bible study, believing this to be unscriptural. I observed how the women hung on every word of one of the male ministerial staff members as he expounded his views. They asked questions, he gave the answer, and nobody challenged anything he said. Although couched in pious terms, the message came through unmistakably—women in the church were there to serve the men. They were granted a few leadership roles, such as supervising preschool or children's Sunday school. Mostly, their areas of service centered on "women's" duties.

This interpretation threw me into turmoil, given the leadership capabilities of my grandmother, mother, and aunts, and their roles in ministry. Not only did it assail my worth as a woman, but also my fledgling identity. Whose interpretation was correct?

What Is Truth?

I remembered the story of Jesus as he stood before Pilate during his so-called trial on charges of blasphemy.

> "You are a king, then!" said Pilate.
> "You are right in saying I am a king. In fact, for this reason I was born, and for this I came into the world, to testify to the truth. Everyone on the side of truth listens to me," Jesus answered.[49]

Pilate expressed his frustration over the strange inner conflict he experienced as the strident demands of the Jewish leaders clashed with his assessment of the man who stood before him.

"What is truth?" he cried out rhetorically and then turned without waiting for an answer and declared Jesus not guilty of being an enemy of the Roman State.

This same question haunted me. Whose "truth" is true? What makes one person's "truth" superior to that of another? Who *can* I believe?

Yet another issue relating to theological interpretation had surfaced. This time I knew enough to draw from a previously untapped resource—the source of wisdom, insight, and understanding.

When I get to heaven, I want to meet and shake hands with all the wise Bereans mentioned in Acts 17. Centuries have passed, but the principle they established holds true. "Now the Berean Jews were of more noble character than those in Thessalonica, for they received the message with great eagerness and examined the Scriptures every day *to see if what Paul said was true"* (italics mine).[50]

A craving for clarification on the role of women in the church drove me to isolate myself at Joan's cottage, armed with a Bible and several books. Gazing out over the calm lake, my mind drifted to those early adventurers who sailed the world in their cramped, corklike vessels. Day after day they floated on a vast sea. The vessel surged forward as wind filled the sails, or it lay becalmed for weeks, even months. Sometimes storms tore at the rigging; other times a brilliant sun beat down, tanning the seamen and bleaching the decks. How did they find their way to their destination? Those sailors plotted their course and recorded progress by means of the fixed, brilliant North Star. They knew they could count on one absolute for guidance and direction.

Jesus wanted to convey to Pilate that in a dark and confusing world, rife with individual interpretation and misinterpretation, he was the lodestar, the guiding principle and ideal. I liked C.S. Lewis' view that the universality of humans meant there were aspects of truth in all religions and cultures. But he contended only Christianity offered *complete* truth.

"Lord Jesus," I prayed. "You said you were the way, the truth, and the life. Now, by your Spirit, please reveal your truth to me on this highly controversial issue."

Jesus was the master communicator and ultimate teacher when he walked on Earth. As I tentatively tested this same ability to get messages through to me, I found it intriguing. Sometimes I stumbled upon a book or heard a chance comment while channel surfing on TV.

Frequently, a scripture leaped off the page, or a friend directed me to a pertinent article. It turned out I had been guided to the right books.

I studied the historical and cultural context surrounding the scriptures used to support arguments against women in ministry leadership and overall attitudes toward women. In ancient Israel, the criteria for leadership and authority were age, gender, and race. You had to be old, you had to be male, and you had to be Hebrew. It was a great system for old Hebrew males. Then the system got blown to pieces at Pentecost when the new basis of authority became evidence of God's Spirit in a person. Attributes like maturity, wisdom, and real knowledge were required.[51]

By the time I left the cottage, I had resolution on the issue. It was a revolutionary exercise. I sought "truth" from the one who said he was Truth—and got a response. This didn't mean I had the definitive answer on the issue, merely sufficient illumination to be at peace.

Heightened Awareness

I returned to the office on Monday and became doubly observant of the interaction between staffers. I found the attitude of male staff members toward female staff members more troubling than the disturbing theological views. They placed enormous emphasis on husbands treating their wives "according to scripture" (loving, respecting, and caring for them), but it didn't seem to go beyond the marriage partnership. Non-wives and female non-family members were often treated as a step up from indentured slaves. I wondered where single (unprotected) women fit into the work of the modern evangelical church. I felt demeaned.

Spiritual abuse is a real phenomenon that actually happens in the church. "It is a subtle trap in which the ones who perpetrate spiritual abuse on others are just as trapped in their unhealthy beliefs and actions as those whom they, knowingly or unknowingly, abuse."[52]

I found it consoling to remember that nearly two thousand years ago the Apostles Peter and Paul had a major disagreement over "theological interpretation." The Jewish leaders held that the ordinance of circumcision was required before non-Jews could fully participate in the fledgling "Church." Peter leaned in that direction, prompting Paul to confront him on the issue. He contended the Jewish church leaders were adding an unnecessary requirement to the free gift of God's grace. In his letter to the Galatians, Paul eloquently and convincingly points out the danger of "grace plus" theology.

A century ago, Grandmother Connie was denied participation in Holy Communion because she did not fulfill the denomination's membership requirement. She was so incensed at what she termed "the traditions of men" that she turned away from the traditional church.

Several years ago I sat in a church service and heard the minister say the Lord's Table was open to "believers who are members in good standing of an evangelical church." Those who could not meet this requirement were asked to pass the elements. I was not a member in good standing of any church at the time. Yet, with a clear conscience and grateful heart, I partook of the sacraments. I hope the church leaders forgave me.

Not much has changed in the organized church over the years. I realize it will always be susceptible to the dictates of its governing powers, the hazards of individual interpretation, and the perils of human fallibility.

It is a challenge to find a church home, more so for those of us who do not fit the norm of "married with children." Or who have little interest in the consuming goal of singles groups—finding a mate. Or who crave hearing the poetry and theology of the old, traditional hymns. But I attend, worship, listen, and participate as led in instances when the church is being the church—Christ's arm of ministry in the world.

POINTER: Wisdom School Has Open Enrollment

- Although free, it's costly. However, the course material, once learned, will revolutionize your life.

- Read Proverbs 2 again and spend time contemplating the promises related to seeking wisdom.

- Set aside any confusion with the modern church and turn to Jesus in prayer for guidance and answers to questions or issues that concern you. He said he was "The Truth."

- The faculty of Wisdom School specializes in communication! Open your mind to what, and how, the Spirit will speak to you.

POINTER REFLECTIONS:

19

OTHERS' EXPECTATIONS OF ME

In order to see Christianity, one must forget almost all the Christians.

—Henri Frédéric Amiel

After the fiasco at the church, I decided against working in a ministry. I had learned valuable lessons through the hurtful experiences but did not want a repeat performance. By now I had a taste of spiritual freedom. The religious trappings were falling away, and my connection to God had strengthened.

My next three jobs were with Christian organizations. I speculated I might find my niche if I combined the professional and Christian environments. God graciously opened each door, and I bettered myself financially and expanded my expertise. But I continued to struggle relationally. My greatest professional strength was the ability to see the big picture and put the pieces together, which worked well when given freedom to exercise this capability. It worked powerfully against me when stifled. Not only did I attempt to measure up to the Christian code of conduct programmed into my thinking, but I looked for and expected it in others. Conflict resulted.

The "Christian" Box

I chafed under the tendency among Christians to put God and other Christians in a box. God did things a certain way; Christians were supposed to do things a certain way. Every time I sneaked my hand out of the "box," someone rapped my knuckles. Occasionally, I allowed my head to pop up in order to take a good hard look at what was going on around me, only to have the lid slammed. I was expected to operate within the framework designed by the leadership. Mixed signals and contradictory messages drove me to distraction.

Sifting through the confusion that existed in evangelical, Christian-based organizations was a huge challenge. I found religious beliefs mingled with workplace expectations, like a huge pot with ingredients thrown in. Each new stir surfaced some unanticipated notion. Praised for exercising initiative and getting the job done, I then faced criticism for not having a "servant attitude" when I set standards and established procedures or spoke up in defense of my staff and peers. Dissension would not be tolerated—it disrupted unity. Image was everything, to be preserved at all costs. Staff members were expected to exhibit the "attitude of Jesus," as defined by the respective leaders.

While Jesus taught that I should honor those in authority over me, he also set the example of leadership.

He demonstrated unfailing patience with his "charges"—his disciples. He never mandated trust and respect—he earned it. He worked with the raw material of individuals and endeavored to bring out the best in each. He didn't drive people, he led them. Jesus recognized human frailty and fallibility; he did not hold up unrealistic standards and feel obligated to point out any and all failings.

It was devastating to observe Christian ministries and organizations assume the role of "holy law enforcement officer" in the lives of employees. Instead of providing an environment in which individuals had the freedom to exercise their God-given abilities, staff members were placed under a microscope. Many women have related stories of disillusionment and confusion as Christian leaders, male and female, crushed their spirits and weakened their spiritual life through wielding power in an inappropriate manner.

I would never for a moment even hint that I was the perfect example of Christian womanhood through all my experiences. Without realizing it, I still carried a void in me and looked to others to fill it. I tried hard to get approval and acceptance by diligent work and endeavoring to help carry the load. When my efforts went unnoticed, it undermined my sense of identity and self-worth.

My struggle with the issues of the Christian church and Christians in particular caused me to distance myself. I had to fight against withdrawing completely. Fortunately, scattered in each of the workplace situations, I encountered some wonderful Christians, those who were growing spiritually—true Christians and shining examples of discipleship. I found friends who prayed with me and offered love and support.

I was back to the concept of the "two" churches—the Church of Jesus Christ comprised of his disciples (believers), and the earthly, organized church comprised of a motley assortment of people and beliefs. I had to accept there was no telling what I might find in the organized Christian church, or among those who professed to be "Christian." Many people drifted in and joined for social standing or community activities, others for business contacts. Still others were put there by the Deceiver to cause confusion and disruption.[53] Each individual brought personal, spiritual, and emotional baggage. Some received the benefit of sound theological teaching; others were taught how to act like a good Christian. Many were content with a weekly motivational shot or a good dose of Christian entertainment. These people then spilled over into the Christian workplace.

It was wonderful to meet someone new and instantly connect because of an awareness of the indwelling presence of Christ, something that could not be faked. If the spiritual dynamic was there, I could rely on God to iron out the kinks in an individual's life as patiently and compassionately as He had done in mine. The more I understood about the graciousness of God in His dealings with me, the more I could extend grace to others.

Whatever happens in the future, I will never again allow the church or other Christians to encroach on my relationship with God. As long as my will rests on my support column, whatever goes on in the religious world is secondary, unrelated to my personal, vital, vertical connection to Him.

Another obstacle between God and me had been removed. The path was clearer than ever. I learned to develop a healthy, realistic view of *Others*. However, all these relationships suggested distance. The course material was notched up as I moved to a deeper level of interaction.

POINTER: Christians Don't Do Well On Pedestals

- Have you ever been hurt or disillusioned by religious leaders or other professing Christians? If so, can you recall specific circumstances?

- Have you tried to distinguish between the vertical connection to God and the horizontal connection to the organized church? When Jesus spoke about building his "kingdom," he referred to residence and rule in the hearts of people. The degree of this is never static.

Loving my neighbor means:
- Recognizing and accepting human imperfections and foibles—and seeing others through the lens of God's amazing grace.
- Fixing my spiritual focus on my support column.
- Applying Skill for Living lessons in my interaction with others.

POINTER REFLECTIONS:

20
MY EXPECTATIONS OF *OTHERS*

If life becomes hard to bear, we think of a change in our circumstances. But the most important and effective change, a change in our own attitude, hardly ever occurs to us, and the resolution to take such a step is very difficult for us.
—Ludwig Wittgenstein

I had an abysmal track record in the area of close, personal relationships. Without realizing it, a tape ran in the back of my mind each time I met an attractive man. "I have a lot of terrific inner needs and inner emptiness and debts to pay, and I'm going to give you a marvelous opportunity to fill my Grand Canyon and take care of me. Aren't I wonderful?"*

My friendships were pleasant, but superficial. Nobody really knew me, not even my parents. My friend

---

and mentor, Joan, had hammered on my protective walls until a crack developed, at least in regard to her. Yet our conversations revolved around spiritual issues. Anything deeply personal remained locked inside.

Emotions drove my behavior, and these see-sawed perilously. An overemphasis on others stifled my fledgling identity and increased my vulnerability to further hurt. Brooding self-absorption led me down a destructive path. I understood that emotional health hinged on achieving a balance between the two, but successfully putting theory into practice eluded me. Although I craved a relationship, the mental picture of my heart once more lying squashed and bleeding on the floor sent me scurrying back into my protective shell. Amanda McBroom's words in "The Rose" accurately summarized the war between my fears and my longing. My heart was so afraid of breaking it had never learned to dance. My journal recorded my feelings:

> I'm tired of trying so hard to build rela-
> tionships and getting little in return. Most
> of all, I am tired of needing companion-
> ship. What is it about me that makes me so
> needy when others apparently are not?

I remembered someone saying, "You never know God is enough until He's all you've got." In my mind, however, an invisible God was inadequate to meet my deepest needs. I wanted someone with skin on. The idea of marriage had drifted to the edges of my mind, probably because I had no man in my life, or on the horizon, or even waiting on some distant cloud. Yet I wasn't designed to live like an island. I knew God could compensate by sending people into my life to help fill the void. Inexplicably, every attempt to reach out for a deeper relationship went awry. Where did the answer lie? Did I simply resign myself to my fate?

Resignation or Acceptance?

I slipped easily into a mindset of resignation. God was God, I was not. His ways were beyond me. If He ordained this life for me, I guessed I should humbly submit to His will. I would make a valiant effort to resign myself to circumstances and try to exhibit the virtues Jesus desired. A noble, martyrlike approach.

Then I read that resignation is sterile, but acceptance is creative. Active acceptance carried the element of hope. My circumstances might be bleak, my past might have generated enormous confusion, yet I could hope. Passive resignation had to go. It wasn't over yet. God could still bring good out of the confusion.

The Psalmist David painted a calming word picture in Psalm 131: "Surely I have composed and quieted my soul; like a weaned child rests against his mother, my soul is like a weaned child within me."[54] I could go on whining and bewailing my struggle to live with unfulfilled needs and appetites, or I could cease being demanding and "compose my soul."

I continued reading, yet it was like learning to swim in a classroom. I might study the mechanics, practice the strokes, and be alerted to the dangers, but swimming would remain a theory. To swim you have to get into the water.

The course material in Skill for Living now called for action. I faced a choice: open my mind and heart to learning about healthy relationships or stay walled up in lonely isolation, nursing my hurts. My innermost being cried out for life, feeling, and freedom.

Venturing Into Vulnerability

February fog covered the mountain in north Georgia when I pulled the car up to the cottage that was to be my home for the weekend. The weather matched my gloomy mood. I wouldn't have come to the women's retreat except a kind friend, knowing my limited financial resources at the time, had invited me to be her guest. Inside I met the other occupants, including a whirlwind named Jacque. Confident, sophisticated, extroverted, she filled the cottage with her presence and epitomized everything I was not.

Summoning my social skills, I joined the group gathered around the kitchen table and found myself seated next to Jacque. Curious about my South African accent, she began asking questions. When the subject of religious upbringing surfaced, the conversation took off as we shared experiences that were surprisingly similar despite being on different continents. I detected an intelligent, lively mind behind eyes that momentarily clouded during our reminiscences. Our spirits connected in that brief conversation, but neither of us realized it then.

Jacque and I lived two miles apart, and although we had good intentions, we didn't manage to schedule a meeting. Her life was full, with nursing, tennis, and a multitude of social activities; mine limped along as I tried to find my own path. On the surface, there didn't appear to be much hope for any level of friendship.

We met again at the retreat reunion six months later. My comment that I needed help with my writing sparked the teacher in Jacque, and she invited me to her elegant home for lunch. The stated purpose was to discuss my work, but the conversation covered a broad range of topics. We agreed to meet socially.

It wasn't easy finding mutually enjoyable activities, given that our tastes were different. She was a party-goer and loved entertaining. Both of these were akin to torture for me. But when we sat over a meal and the conversation turned to books, upbringing, or theology, we connected.

Those first few months of friendship were rough as I groped my way into the tangled, thorny underbrush of relationships. I was a classic VDP—Very Draining Person—to anyone who made overtures of friendship.

We related well on a spiritual level, but I found her insufferably independent and inscrutable. She got frustrated at her inability to penetrate my emotional walls and impatient with what she sensed was my dependency. The odds were not good for a long-term friendship.

Time passed. Jacque pursued her interests, including several men, and I plodded along. Then one revealing conversation about her childhood touched me deeply and gave me insight that forever changed my thinking about her. I wanted to reach out to her in some way but was not comfortable doing this verbally. So I wrote a note. In it I stated that our paths may diverge, there would be misunderstandings, hurt feelings, confusing behavior, but I wanted to be a friend to her. In return, I asked that she make me talk, make me open up and verbalize long-buried feelings. I needed someone trustworthy to help me break down the walls. Jacque turned out to be a master at this.

Our friendship moved to a different level at that time. She found in me an empathetic, accepting listener. I discovered someone who "read" me like nobody had before. Without conscious awareness, we began nurturing each other's spirit. What developed was a symbiotic friendship that God used in our lives as we shared lessons along the way.

Despite my difficulties in this area, I made a commitment to hang on. I needed a starting point in my quest to learn about relationships, and Jacque offered an opportunity, boundaries to bounce against. With her solid theological background and sensitive caring, she became a source of stability in a time of emotional and spiritual turbulence. God brought the right support alongside.

I continued to pray for wisdom, insight, and understanding. My journal records another piercing flash of illumination as I reflected on the three areas of temptation—sex, power, and money.

> I knew that power was not a temptation for me. Money wasn't really either, as I'm not driven to make or hoard money, although lack of money affects my sense of security. Sex, of itself, is not a temptation. I decided long ago that sex outside of

marriage was not an option. Sex without the emotional support and stability of a committed relationship would shatter me into a million pieces. I could not risk that. Besides, nobody died of abstinence.

But as I analyzed what sex represented, I realized my temptation is the intimacy, closeness, and sense of belonging associated with sex and emotions. This is a seductive pull. I have to be honest and acknowledge that if there were someone in my life who gave me these feelings, I would become putty in their hands. I run the risk of submerging my identity in theirs in order to get what I crave. It's like having an addiction.

Three months later I met a woman at work, I'll call her Pat. She exuded self-confidence, which I found refreshing. We discovered a surprising level of compatibility, sparking each other's wit and then laughing to the point of tears. Without realizing it, I slipped into my submissive "putty" behavior, content to drift along in her wake, desperate to please. My mind never made the connection to the similarity of my past behavior with men, and I stifled any qualms about the imbalance in our roles.

Yet the One orchestrating my circumstances wasn't about to let me be detoured. I had chosen the path that I believed could lead to spiritual freedom and emotional health—and I was only part way along it.

I now faced the next component of my equal-arm balance model—*Self.* To ignore this pan would leave me with a lopsided scale.

POINTER: Human Relationships Enhance Life; They Were Never Meant to Fill the God-Shaped Void

- What, or who, are your most important relationships?

- Are you looking for someone to enhance your life—or fill it?

- Have you ever considered what inner needs may be driving your behavior?

POINTER REFLECTIONS:

PART SEVEN

THE SUSPENDED PAN OF *SELF*

21
DEFINING *SELF*

Love for self is as necessary for maturity and wholeness and holiness as is love for God and for other people.
—David A. Seamands

I don't like roller-coaster rides and cannot fathom the appeal of having my stomach dislodged, swallowing my heart, and paying for the privilege. A water log ride is about my speed. Nevertheless, there have been times when I plucked up the courage to go on something more daring. I sit buckled in my seat, my anxiety mounting as we climb higher and the top of the loop inexorably creeps closer. Soon we are over the crest, and I am hanging on for dear life as we zoom down, only to have to face the same cycle again. By then I have decided this wasn't a good idea, and I want to stop the process—and I can't. I am committed to seeing it through to the end and can only trust that I will emerge in one piece and walking upright.

I felt much the same way as I approached examining *Self.* I would have preferred to limit my exploration to the scope of *God* and *Others.* These two areas had been challenging enough. I knew the lessons learned up to this point had proved enormously beneficial, but they had also been excruciating. The suspicion lurked in my mind that looking at *Self* would entail more pain. Yet to validate the theory of the weighing scale model, I was compelled to examine this component. To not do so presented a picture of an out-of-balance scale.

I had looked at the roots of my concept of God. Now it was time to look at the experiences, conversations, incidents, sermons, and hidden messages that comprised my past. I mentally fastened my seat belt and set off on the ride.

Confusion Over *Self*

My mother adopted Grandpa Archie's literal interpretation of scripture. She often quoted Jesus' words, "If any man will come after me, let him deny himself, and take up his cross, and follow me."[55] "Deny himself" meant just that. It was self-centered and unspiritual to focus on personal needs or wants. This tied into her passion for service to others.

From my frame of reference, *Self* related to the sinful nature spoken of in scripture.[56] It implied selfishness, following baser appetites, and excluding God. Mom took this further and applied literal interpretation of a verse in Galatians to her own self-concept: "For if a man think himself to be something, when he is nothing, he deceiveth himself."[57]

I picked up the message that negating my wants equaled Godly and parental approval. Doing the "right" thing became ingrained in my psyche. Countless sermons over the years intensified my confusion. The "flesh"—my humanness—always carried a negative implication. Emotions other than happy, positive ones were linked to my "flesh." Expressions of anger, fear, doubt, depression stemmed from my choice to operate in my "flesh."

A journal entry revealed my continuing confusion on the subject of *Self*. I read a scripture in Hebrews: "Therefore, since we are surrounded by such a great cloud of witnesses, let us throw off everything that hinders and the sin that so easily entangles. And let us run with perseverance the race marked out for us."[58] It is interesting to look back now and see how my thought pattern immediately focused on the "sin that so easily entangles" (the negative). The other part of the verse is equally significant and has a different connotation ". . . run with perseverance the race marked out for us." The implication in the words is that our race is custom-designed for us individually. It emphasizes the positive.

Nevertheless, at the time I wrote, "I also realized that I needed to work at dealing with the 'sin which so easily entangles me,'—my battle with depression, my past, brooding over my emotional state and my deep hurts. In the same way I overcame doubt by a deliberate decision, I need to concentrate on aspiring to emotional healing."

In this brief statement I unwittingly stumbled on a teaching that causes enormous conflict among those suffering from emotional difficulties and generates huge controversy in theological circles.

Many pastors and lay Christian counselors tend to place a major portion of the blame for personality and emotional problems on "sin" in an individual's life—not necessarily the dark and dreadful sins, but the "sins" of self-righteousness, pride, self-pity, and other expressions of the "flesh." The message conveyed is take care of the sin issue through confession and the application of scripture, and the psychological difficulties will automatically be addressed.

I was clear on the theological issue, that we receive God's gift of salvation by His grace—spiritual. However, I picked up the subtext message that we then work hard at *maintaining* that salvation through our good deeds and exemplary living—behavioral—avoiding the "sins that entangle."

The Biblical Counseling Model

My quest for answers prompted me to investigate a counseling approach called Nouthetic counseling, or "Biblical counseling," developed by Jay E. Adams and promoted in many churches.

> To put it simply, nouthetic counseling consists of lovingly confronting people out of deep concern in order to help them make those changes that God requires. By confrontation we mean that one Christian personally gives counsel to another from the Scriptures. [...] By change we mean that counseling is done because there is something in another Christian's life that fails to meet the Biblical requirements and that, therefore, keeps him from honoring God. All counseling—Biblical or otherwise—attempts change.[59]

While the above raised questions in my mind, I did not want to jump to hasty conclusions, so I studied further. In *How To Help People Change*, Adams elaborates on the basis for his counseling model: the infallibility and inerrancy of the scriptures.

Mom obviously practiced "nouthetic counseling," even though she had never heard the term. Grandpa Archie and Grandma Connie had drilled into her the belief that the only source for instruction and guidance was the Bible. My sister and I were given scriptural "counseling" in response to any and every situation, to the point where we rolled our eyes and teased Mom by saying, "Oh, dear, here comes sermon number 2,374,596!" I got "nouthetic counseling" whenever I slumped into one of my down moods. She firmly believed the application of scripture could "fix" whatever might be wrong with me.

The Infallibility of the Interpreter?

Although I accept and believe in the infallibility and adequacy of the scriptures, my experiences painfully showed that when humans are the avenues of interpretation, the door to misunderstanding is flung wide open. My own early interpretation of Psalm 84:11 is a perfect illustration, "No good thing does He withhold from those who walk uprightly." Someone trying to emphasize God's goodness and generosity may encourage another by saying, "No good *thing* does He withhold from those who walk uprightly"—be it marriage, a child, a fabulous job, or any other worthy gift. But someone who has learned to understand God's "No" could apply the same scripture with an entirely different meaning, "No *good* thing does He withhold from those who walk uprightly." The scripture is identical—the interpretation to the "counselee" vastly different.

Scripture, and its application, had been my guiding light for most of my life. However, I also recognized I had fallen into the trap of placing my own interpretation upon the verses. As I pondered the subject of "Biblical counseling," I again faced the core issue of "Whose truth is true?" That there is bad interpretation is unquestioned. Jacque's classic line expressed my sentiments, "I believe in the infallibility of the scriptures. I do not believe in the infallibility of the people interpreting the scriptures." The last thing I wanted was to go haring off down another blind alley. This was too crucial.

How did I separate the good from the bad? I needed insight from the source of truth, my "North Star." I prayed the Spirit would reveal truth to me on this issue. He did. Not by writing on the wall, but by bringing to my attention a story which touched a raw nerve.

I heard about two adults engaged in conversation in a parking lot outside a nursing home. A boy aged about seven and a girl about nine accompanied one speaker. The children waited patiently as the adults conversed and then, as frequently happens, nature called. The boy began to squirm and interrupted his father.

"Daddy, I have to pee."

Getting back into the locked Alzheimer's unit presented a challenge, so the father told his son he would have to wait until they got home. The boy's discomfort grew as the conversation between the adults continued. In desperation, he disappeared behind the cars, unzipped his pants, and relieved himself. By this time, the girl had heard the same call of nature.

"Daddy, I have to pee," she said, tugging on his sleeve.

The father told her she, too, would have to wait until they got home. They both knew she did not have the advantage her brother had.

"But I can't, Daddy. I have to go real bad," she protested.

"No, honey, you must wait. You know what the Bible says, 'I can do all things through Christ who strengthens me.'"

I wish this were fabricated, but it's not. Talk about misinterpretation of scripture! I can only imagine the confusion generated in the girl's mind.

A New Twist on an Old Theme

My mind drifted back almost a hundred years. I reflected on Grandpa Archie's and Grandma Connie's literal interpretation of scripture, specifically, "Jesus Christ is the same yesterday and today and forever."[60] They knew Jesus went about healing physical suffering and performing miracles of provision. In their minds, then, if he truly had not changed, the application of his Word was sufficient to generate similar healings and provision in their day.

The story of Mom's appendicitis attack and her "miraculous" healing had become a jewel in the family. Grandma Connie's actual account follows:

Dorothy took very ill when she was about twelve years of age, with a severe attack of appendicitis. Lying in my room, I was keeping watch over her, and about the middle of the night I heard her speaking and realized she was doing so in her sleep. I bent over her and this is what I heard her say: "It is better for us to break down this old house and go to another house where there will never be any sickness." This brought to my mind the words of Paul in 2 Corinthians 5:1, "If the earthly house of this Tabernacle were dissolved, we have a building of God, an house not made with hands, eternal in the Heavens."

I then fully realized that we were facing a fight for her life. She grew worse daily, and no matter how we prayed, there came only temporary relief and no permanent healing. She suffered intense pain, but strange to say, after each attack, in a low but very clear voice, she sang a hymn... and a number of other hymns, as these spasms of pain came quite frequently. On the fourth day she was worse than ever, her temperature was rising, and the appendix fearfully distended, and so tender to the touch that she could not straighten out her right leg or bear the slightest pressure, not even that of a soft blanket. There were clear evidences of the inflammation spreading.

Our faith was sorely tested, but in our hearts we were assured that our dear Lord was with us and our prayers were not unheard by Him, and if we believe that He hears us, then we have the petition that we desired of Him. The greatest test I was feeling was I knew in my heart that the Lord wanted me to be willing to surrender her altogether to Him. I kept this to myself, and later on my husband came to me and said, "Do you realize that God wants you and me to part with Dorothy?" I replied, "Yes, and only for two reasons would I be willing to do so, and these are: If she goes now, I know she is saved, but I do not know what she will be like later on in life—only He knows. The other reason is: God knows her future and may want to take her home now to save her from something worse." In my heart I was willing. But, oh, only God knows what it meant to me to say, "Yes, Lord!"

Just then she called to us, and when we reached the bed she said, "Daddy, I'm sinking. I feel so light as if I am not on the bed." Then came another fearful spasm of pain that made her scream.

It was about 9:00 p.m. and we agreed to call in a doctor. We knew her condition was critical and the law demanded our having a physician in case of death. At 9:30 p.m. he came, and after thoroughly examining her, he turned to us and said, "This is a case of acute appendicitis and her chances of lasting through this night are very remote. She must be removed to the hospital for an immediate operation." This doctor knew the views we held, but he hoped we would not decline to have her operated on, for it was the only advice he could give us. We thanked him and he left.

What we experienced that night was dreadful! Successive spasms of intense pain would be followed by the plaintive singing of a hymn. But we kept our eyes on the Lord Jesus, our mighty physician. Early the next morning we gathered round the bedside and again lifted our hearts to God in earnest prayer. A few minutes later, Dorothy suddenly exclaimed, "All pain is gone! I am healed!" Praise God, we found once again that it is true that "He will not allow us to be tempted above what we are able to bear." After a few hours she could straighten her leg and sit up. Propped up by pillows, she was playing with her dolls, and a couple of days later she was out of bed. Many years have passed since the wonderful healing and she has never had a sign of appendix trouble.

The test was severe, but His Grace was stronger. He surely is the same yesterday, today and forever!

I cried when I read this, yet sadly it is a perfect illustration of the dangers inherent in the misinterpretation and misapplication of scripture, the imposition of another's will in the guise of spiritual instruction, and a distorted view of God's dealings. It is highly likely that Mom's appendix burst, thereby relieving the pain. The miracle is the fact she did not die from the result.

As this story illustrates, those early Pentecostals adopted the stance that God's Word alone was sufficient for every circumstance, especially in the realm of physical healing. To resort to "modern medicine" as an aid in healing was a statement against the sufficiency and adequacy of God to meet the need.

A hundred years later, Biblical counselors are applying the same thinking in the area of emotional healing. To resort to "modern psychology" as an aid in healing is a statement against the sufficiency of God to meet the need. Inappropriately applying scripture to a physical need is cruel. It is equally cruel to inappropriately apply scripture to an emotional need.

This was a dead-end trail. Nouthetic counseling hadn't helped in the past. Now it threw me back into the "spiritual self/behavioral self" quandary.

I needed to look in another direction.

POINTER: Consider the Origins of Your View of *Self*

- What emotions surface?

- Do you view "self" as being selfish, egotistical, or unspiritual?

- Do you find you are harder on yourself than on others?

- Has the "Christian" concept of emphasis on loving others overshadowed the need to know and love yourself appropriately?

POINTER REFLECTIONS:

22
TWO *SELFS?*

The author who benefits you most is not the one who tells you something you did not know before, but the one who gives expression to the truth that has been dumbly struggling in you for utterance.

—Oswald Chambers

In 1995 my Skill for Living Instructor threw me a lifeline by inspiring Jacque to give me *Healing Your Heart of Painful Emotions,* a compendium of four books by David A. Seamands. This time, instead of the feeling of a dentist's drill on a raw nerve generated by the Biblical counseling model, I experienced a sense of gasping a lung full of air after being under water for a long time.

This author took a different counseling position. He wrote that preachers often give people the mistaken idea becoming a Christian will automatically take care of emotional hang-ups and contended this was not true. "A great crisis experience of Jesus Christ, as important and eternally valuable as this is, is not a shortcut to emotional health. It is not a quickie cure for personality problems."*

What a liberating thought! My emotional problems did not necessarily stem from "sin" or not being in right standing with God. The two were separate.

There was no doubt my spiritual self had strengthened as I gained confidence in God, my support column. My behavioral self, however, continued to bump along on the bottom, struggling with perfectionism, intensely aware of inadequacies in relationships. These two aspects of *Self* were deeply entwined in my thinking, like an overgrown vine on an aged tree. David Seamands gave me permission to separate my spiritual self from my behavioral self.

To my delight, I found a whole chapter on self in *Putting Away Childish Things*. Seamands wrote that Christians will readily toss about terms like self-surrender, complete consecration, crucifixion of the self. Yet a proper understanding of these concepts is central to the Christian life. He stated:

> If you have the wrong mental map of self and of self-surrender, your Christian life will surely end in despair and disillusionment. No concept is more important to a mature understanding of what Christ is asking from you. [. . .] The Far East tries to solve the problem of self by getting rid of it.

Buddhism says, "Snuff out the candle of self: Nirvana." Hinduism goes at it a little more gently: not self-extinction, but self-absorption into God. The personal, individual selfhood is to be so united with God that it is like a raindrop falling back into the ocean from whence it came, losing its own identity.*

But when the Apostle Paul stated that he was "crucified with Christ," he wasn't saying he was dead. He understood his essential self was still alive. He hadn't been destroyed, absorbed, or dissolved. Seamands continues:

The Christian faith does not have the slightest hint in it that your selfhood or mine will be extinguished when we get [to heaven]. Forever fix in your mind that your ego comes from God Himself and that selfhood is eternal, imperishable, and indestructible. God does not desire to destroy it. He can fellowship with it and reward it in a heaven; He can isolate it and separate Himself from it in a hell. But it persists.*

Seamands then addresses the issue of self-disparagement:

---

*David A. Seamands, *Putting Away Childish Things*, Indianapolis, IN: Light and Life Communications, 1999, pp. 109-111. Used by permission.

It is dangerous to think of self as something detached and essentially evil. Jesus said that we should love God with our whole hearts and love our neighbor as we love ourselves. Love for self is as necessary for maturity and wholeness and holiness as is love for God and for other people. Indeed, loving God and loving my neighbor require a measure of self-acceptance and self-love in which I hold my own selfhood in esteem, integrity, identity, and respect.[*]

Then I read a statement that shone a spotlight into the deep quagmire of my relational difficulties:

Self-love, not selflessness, is the basis of interpersonal relationships. Selflessness between people can turn out to be mere compliance and appeasement. It is often used to rationalize copping out on the tough, real-life questions of right and wrong. And, of course, selflessness in the hands of a Christian bully can become an exquisite instrument of torture, of spiritual and emotional blackmail. If he can make you feel guilty by saying to you, "You're thinking about yourself," then

---

[*]David A. Seamands, *Putting Away Childish Things*, Indianapolis, IN: Light and Life Communications, 1999, p. 112. Used by permission.

he can control and manipulate you into
doing whatever he wants.*

Such thinking opens the door to spiritual and emotional abuse.

Looking again at Jay Adams's approach, I read: "The Nouthetic counselor believes that all that is needed to help another person love God and his neighbor as he should . . . may be found in the Bible."[61]

Since I was exploring the root of God's instructions to the Israelites in the Ten Commandments, I found the omission of love of *Self* significant. While Jesus makes reference to two commandments, the second commandment has two parts: love your neighbor, love yourself. Eliminating "love of *Self*" reveals the divergence between the two counseling paths.

I was beginning to understand that the heartbeat of the Christian life is love: loving God with my whole self, and then loving others as I love myself. My difficulty lay in the interpretation I had absorbed. Jesus instructed me to "Love your neighbor as you love yourself," not love my neighbor instead of myself.[62] The idea conveys a healthy self-love, functioning appropriately and overflowing to others.

But to me this was like aiming at the flag on a golf green when you know your best efforts are doing little more than stirring up sand, filling the ponds with golf balls, and frightening the birds in the woods. Obviously, more Skill for Living lessons were needed.

In *Healing for Damaged Emotions,* Seamands stated that some of the most powerful weapons in Satan's arsenal are psychological. He lists fear, doubt, anger, hostility, worry—all of which plagued me. Then he hit the nail squarely on the head when he added guilt. I excelled at guilt. An incident that someone else would airily dismiss as being of no consequence sent me careening off balance.

> Satan's greatest psychological weapon is a gut-level feeling of inferiority, inadequacy, and low self-worth. This feeling shackles many Christians, in spite of wonderful spiritual experiences, in spite of their faith and knowledge of God's Word. Although they understand their position as sons and daughters of God, they are tied up in knots, bound by a terrible feeling of inferiority, and chained to a deep sense of worthlessness.*

Seamands went on to describe how low self-esteem paralyzed potential, destroyed dreams, ruined relationships, and sabotaged Christian service.

With blinding clarity, I realized the missing element—the positive meaning of *Self,* my basic personhood, the *Self* God intended me to be. The singular "me" with all the possibilities for my individual personality with its talents and gifts. God, who can't even stand

---

*©1981, 2008 Cook Communications Ministries. *Healing for Damaged Emotions* by David A. Seamands. Used with permission. May not be further reproduced. All rights reserved.

to make two snowflakes alike, made me to be uniquely myself.

Where did it all go wrong? Again, Seamands shone the light of insight into my darkened mind:

> One of the characteristics of the child is that he knows and understands things partially. Part of growing up into mature love is to reach a fuller, face-to-face understanding. Our pictures and our feelings we see reflected in our family members— what we watch in their expressions, hear from the tone in their voices, and see from their actions. These reflections tell us not only who we are, but also what we are going to become. As the reflections gradually become part of us, we take on the shape of the person we see in the family looking glass.[*]

The weight in my heart lifted slightly as I realized I wasn't alone in my struggle to sort out the spiritual versus the behavioral. The author had himself battled the effects of childhood programming. Many books have been written about negative influences in formative years, but this time the author shared openly that his programming came from within the context of a Christian missionary family. He used the illustration of how the rings of a giant sequoia tree reveal its develop-

---

mental history, year by year. Drought, too much rain, lightning, a forest fire, blight and disease, interspersed by years of normal growth, all lie embedded in the heart of the tree.

> That's the way it is with us. Just a few thin layers beneath the protective bark—the concealing, protective mask—are the recorded rings of our lives.
> There are scars of ancient, painful hurts ...
> Here is the discoloration of a tragic stain that muddied all of life . . .
> And here we see the pressure of a painful, repressed memory . . .
> In the rings of our thoughts and emotions, the record is there; the memories are recorded, and all are alive. And they directly and deeply affect our concepts, our feelings, and our relationships. They affect the way we look at life and God, at others and ourselves.[*]

My daily prayer for wisdom led me to the inescapable conclusion that, like it or not, I was going to have to delve into my emotional and psychological background, to examine the developmental rings of my own "tree." I had no idea at the time that this exploration would be so wide-ranging it could fill another book.

---

[*]©1981, 2008 Cook Communications Ministries. *Healing for Damaged Emotions* by David A. Seamands. Used with permission. May not be further reproduced. All rights reserved.

POINTER: Whose View of *Self* Dominates Your Thinking?

- Do you agree with David Seamands' definition of *Self*?

- Can you see the benefit of separating your *spiritual self* from your *behavioral self*?

- Do you believe that your *spiritual self* is healthy?

- Describe your spiritual foundation?

- What aspect of your *behavioral self* would you like to change?

POINTER REFLECTIONS:

23
A NEW PERSPECTIVE

So you are no longer slaves, but God's children; and since you are his children, he has made you also heirs.

Galatians 4:7 (TNIV)

In the black-and-white picture I look around three years of age, standing in front of a giant cactus in our yard, wisps of short blond hair waving in the breeze. Dangling from my hand is the infamous basket, an innocuous item in itself, but one that represented a critical turning point in my development.

Trips with Mom to the Indian market were highlights of my childhood. Durban had a large population of Indians who had migrated to South Africa from India to work in the sugar cane fields surrounding the city. The Indians ran the most wonderful open market, filled with smells of fresh, raw vegetables, curry and spices, dry dusty potatoes, with a hint of the betel nut they constantly chewed. Even at the tender age of three other cultures fascinated me. I loved the colors of the saris of the Indian women and stared, fascinated, at the small red dots in the center of their foreheads, indicating their Hindu beliefs. Hawkers standing behind rows of stalls enticed buyers with claims that their wares were the freshest (only occasionally true). Stands of abundant fresh flowers added splashes of brilliant color among the dull beans and onions. It was magical. I never lost my love for the Indian market, and as I grew older, I couldn't wait for school holidays so that I could again go with Mom on this great adventure.

The market was the setting for my first major show of independence. I generally "helped" Mom with her purchases, proudly carrying my small basket as she carried the larger ones. For some reason, on this day I got it into my mind that I wanted to carry eggs. I've no idea why it had to be eggs, except that perhaps eggs represented growth and progress from the safe and uninteresting potatoes I normally carried.

"No, you'll drop them," said Mom.

"No, I won't," I said. "I'll be very careful. Please let me carry some eggs."

Reluctantly, Mom gave in. I happily trotted alongside her, carefully carrying my basket. Whether I tripped, became overconfident, or bumped into something, I have no idea. All I know is a short while later the basket slipped out of my hand, and I gazed horrified at smashed shells and yellow egg yolks spreading messily at my feet.

I can't remember what transpired between Mom and me, but the incident and interaction obviously made a profound impression. Mom told me years later that

I could not be persuaded under any circumstance to carry eggs in my basket again.

"It's All Your Fault"

Much to my humiliation, Dad incorporated the story of me and the eggs into his sermon on God's permissive will. My experience was not presented in a good light. His notes state, "Many people come to God not to obtain His will but His approval of their own plans." What should have been a humorous childhood anecdote on the trials of growing up became a parable of the blackness of the human condition and the dire consequences of willfulness.

I sat in the pew and listened to this sermon several times over the course of the years. Each retelling reinforced in my impressionable mind how foolish I was to have ignored Mom's advice. Obviously my actions revealed poor judgment and a lack of spiritual maturity. God undoubtedly interpreted my actions the same way Dad did. It was the first recording session of the "It's all your fault" message in my mind. Additionally, this introduced an element of tension into my church attendance. I could never be sure if the week's minor childhood infraction would be broadcast from the pulpit.

A Commendable Decision

The year was 1956. I was sixteen, working full time as an entry-level clerk in the bookkeeping department of a fair-sized engineering firm in Durban.

One day we were told the company had arranged for a helicopter to fly clients over the city as a promotional event. As a treat, the staff was invited to share in this great adventure. I had never flown before and found the prospect of a helicopter ride incredibly exciting. My co-workers and I talked with keen anticipation about what to wear, the weather forecast, would we get airsick? There was one major problem. The ride was to take place on a Sunday morning, right during Sunday School time. I faced a huge dilemma.

I told Mom about this once-in-a-lifetime opportunity and the fact that it was scheduled for a Sunday. She did not tell me I could not participate. She did point out that I was in charge of the Beginner Department. Would I be able to find a replacement? She told me to pray about it and make my decision. But a subtle message was conveyed. It really wouldn't set a good example if I missed church and Sunday School to go on a helicopter ride, Sunday being the Lord's Day. The appropriate "spiritual" response would be to "deny myself."

I did pray about the matter. I wanted to do the right thing as a Christian—but oh, how I wanted to go on that helicopter ride. It hooked right into my love of anything associated with travel. Regrettably, God did not give me a revelation in the night as I hoped. Nor did I hear His voice authorizing me to step out of the line of duty. I had the lurking fear that God might punish my "rebellion" and something dreadful would happen.

The aura of expectations and obligations that permeated my home proved too powerful. I caved in to my fear and told my colleagues I would not be joining them. They were aghast at my turning down this opportunity and sensed my deep disappointment. I stoically went off to Sunday School and church on the appointed Sunday and tried not to think about what I was missing—the adventure of the helicopter ride and the chance to slowly hover over my beautiful city, enjoying God's spectacular creation.

Mom and Dad commended me on my "wise" decision. They told me they believed the Lord would honor my commitment to Him and the church. As if to emphasize the principle of "denying self," a couple of months later they gave me my first commercial flight to Port Elizabeth.

I suspect the God I now know would have delighted in seeing the excitement and pleasure of a sixteen-year-old enjoying His gifts and His creation from a never-to-be-forgotten helicopter ride. But at the time, this was a totally foreign concept, one which clearly did not fit with "denial of self." My attention to the "letter of the Law" obscured the loving God behind "the Law."[63]

A New Perspective

Decades later, and for the first time, I opened my mind to critically analyze the effect of these incidents on my development as a person. I was directed to again read *Freedom from the Performance Trap* and discovered the missing link in my thinking—an inaccurate view of myself from God's perspective. David Seamands so beautifully summarized God's view that I immediately excerpted and adapted the author's major points and placed them in my bathroom. Every day I read:

SERVANT OR DAUGHTER?

The **servant** is accepted and appreciated on the basis of what she does, the **daughter** on the basis of who she is.

The **servant** starts the day anxious and worried, wondering if her work will really please her master. The **daughter** rests in the secure love of her family.

The **servant** is accepted because of her workmanship, the **daughter** because of a relationship.

The **servant** is accepted because of her productivity and performance. The **daughter** belongs because of her position as a person.

At the end of the day, the **servant** has peace of mind only if she is sure she has proven her worth by her work. The next morning her anxiety begins again. The **daughter** can be secure all day and know that tomorrow won't change her status.

When a **servant** fails, her whole position is at stake; she might lose her job. When a **daughter** fails, she will be grieved because she has hurt her parents, and she will be corrected and disciplined. But she is not afraid of being thrown out. Her confidence is in belonging and being loved, and her performance does not change the stability of her position. *

---

*David A. Seamands, *Freedom from the Performance Trap,* Victor Books, Div. of Scripture Press Publications, Inc., 1988, p. 22. Used by permission.

I added a personalized version of the verse in Galatians 4:7: "You are not a **servant** any longer; you are a **daughter**. And, if you are a **daughter**, then you are certainly an heir of God through Christ."

As a result of my early programming, I viewed myself solely as God's servant—or, to be more accurate, a lowly grunt among the hordes in God's army. In reality, I was God's child!

My will had to tell my mind to choose to believe this truth, to resolutely switch my thought pattern from servant thinking to daughter thinking. It was abundantly clear that my notoriously unstable emotions could never function as an indicator of God's love and acceptance. Either I believed His word, or I should stop now and forget the whole thing.

I will forever be extremely grateful that my "boot camp" process was gradual and intermittent. The emotional toll of dealing with everything at once would have destroyed me. God, the One who knows me best, paced His lessons according to how He knew I could handle them and timed them to my receptivity. He "knows how we are formed, he remembers that we are dust."[64]

How I wish I could stop right here and conclude my story. Having learned this secret, my struggle ended. My past wounds were erased. Life became joyful, purposeful. The quality of my relationships soared as a result of my newfound knowledge.

Not so. I was about to face a major assault on my mind and my faith.

POINTER: Your View of *Self* Colors Your View of Circumstances, Relationships, and God

- Can you recall specific incidents that shaped your thinking, similar to what happened to me?

- Did subsequent experiences solidify your assessment of yourself?

- If so, how?

- Has anything or anyone caused you to change your mind?

POINTER REFLECTIONS:

PART EIGHT

ADJUSTING THE WEIGHTS

24
A WINDING, ARDUOUS, BATTLE-FILLED PATH

For it is one thing to see the land of peace from a wooded ridge . . . and another to tread the road that leads to it.

—St. Augustine

Freedom is scary. Life is much easier when someone else tells you how to live it—be it the church, religion, parents, spouse, family members, friends, or secular society. Unless handled wisely, freedom from slavery (control) can degenerate into a worse form of bondage. In the twentieth century, the breakup of the former Soviet Union gave many examples of individuals and countries who struggled with the challenges of freedom.

The Israelites had no hint of the training they faced when they set out with such exuberance from Egypt. They, like me, would have crumpled in discouragement had they been given an inkling of what lay ahead.

A major transformation had to take place before they would be ready to conquer and take possession of the land God had promised them.

The path Moses and the people followed on their journey from Egypt to what is now Israel is fascinating. A map of the area shows a much shorter, less circuitous route, traveling directly up the west Mediterranean coast rather than the eastern route along which God led them. This route minimizes time in the heat and sand of the desert.

Historical records tell us that a formidable fighting force guarded the west coast, garrisons of soldiers belonging to the various peoples populating the area. The inhabitants of Canaan were not about to give up their territory simply because the Israelites said that their Yahweh had ordained they take it over. These people were accustomed to defending their cities and property and were prepared to fight any intruders to the finish. If the Israelites wanted to occupy the land, they would have to overcome the "giants" they were so afraid of many years earlier.

These warriors certainly did not present a challenge to the God who had caused the sea to part. The Creator of the universe could have vaporized them. Why didn't He? Why didn't He simply eliminate the obstacles?

The hordes of people shuffling their way through the desert were former slaves, accustomed to blindly following orders. Further, they were not used to looking after themselves. To lead them up against garrisons of well-trained, fierce warriors would be like providing cannon—or arrow—fodder. Rather than miraculously stepping in to smooth their path, God wanted to teach them how to handle the inevitable adversities of life. He planned to turn a ragtag bunch of animal herders into a fighting force capable, under His guidance and direction, of dealing with any enemy.

Considerable preparations and training were needed before this would happen. Moses' assistant, Joshua, was appointed to the position of "General," and boot camp began. God planned that by the time they actually went into battle they would have built confidence in their Commander in Chief—Yahweh Himself—in General Joshua, and in themselves. They would have developed combat skills and weaponry, be equipped to fight, and more importantly, win.

So they took the circuitous route and ambled their way through the wilderness, learning, growing in trust, failing, praising, complaining, and trying to figure out what this new lifestyle of being led by an invisible God was all about.

I found it immeasurably comforting to read how God remained mindful of the physical stamina of the people. Not only did He provide a cloud cover from the burning sun and a pillar of fire to provide warmth and light, but He also paced the journey out of consideration for the children and flocks. The day-to-day circumstances were trying and frequently inexplicable, yet there was no doubt about God's overshadowing presence and care.

And each new day brought another opportunity to experience living free.

God never intended that His people become entangled in religious trappings or the strictures of a society that holds individuals captive by insisting on conformity and mandating how they live. He laid down some basic requirements for relating to Him and gave guidelines for maintaining healthy relationships with *Self* and *Others*. He designed that His children, individually, live a free life under His direction, and He offered instruction on how to appropriately handle true freedom.

I still wished God would instantly transform me, leaving me free to begin a new life. But I, like the Israelites, discovered this is not His way. He is more interested in building strength into the fiber of my being than in eliminating pain and discomfort. God's training program calls for commitment to the course and a willingness to go into battle. Encountering "giants" along the way is inevitable, overcoming them is optional.

One major giant in my life had been "slain"—the organized church. But there were others.

Fresh Resolve

Some time ago, my sister gave me a funny little paper double-disc with a rubber band hooked through the top. On it were the words, "World's Greatest Goal Setter." Obviously she had concluded this was not my greatest strength!

At the beginning of 2000, I decided to set goals for the year:

- I will finally put my past and its erroneous programming behind me. I will not allow myself to slide back into old thought patterns.
- I will continue to grow in all aspects of wisdom: skill in living, insight, and understanding.
- I will monitor my physical and emotional resources, quickly become aware when my reserves are getting low, and take appropriate action.
- I will strive to develop an attitude of "reckless abandon" about my future, resting in the assurance that God undertakes to guide the future as He has the past.

I started exercising the power of my will.

Then came a devastating blow. On February 24, 2000, I received a phone call from Joan's daughter-in-law. My beloved friend and mentor had dropped dead at the lunch table in a restaurant. Stunned, I retreated to the solace of my home and reflected on our friendship. Joan had given me the inestimable gift of companionship and unconditional acceptance. I found her always ready to listen, constantly encouraging yet challenging, consistently pointing me to a loving Heavenly Father. Her calm presence and rock-steady friendship stabilized me through years of turmoil. Now she was gone.

At Joan's funeral, I asked her daughter for the plaque that had hung on the wall of her home: "*God gives the best to those who leave the choice to Him.*" Joan believed and practiced this, developing a confident trust in the care of a trustworthy God.

In the following weeks and months, feelings of loss engulfed me at intermittent periods. If only I could pick up the phone one more time to chat with her. Death was so dreadfully final. I had few really important relationships, and now a main pillar of support had gone forever. The pattern of my life seemed to be one loss after another, with diminishing sources of love and caring. My glass tilted back to the "half empty" view. Fear of repeating the pain of the past immobilized me. I looked at the future through a dark lens and saw only escalating aloneness. Then the Spirit gently reminded me, "Joy, look at Job in the Bible. He suffered tremendous losses and pain, but this didn't last forever. It was for a time and a purpose." I thought of the comforting words in Ecclesiastes 3, "There is a time for everything."

The following Sunday we sang a wonderful old hymn about the love of Jesus—love like no other love. I mourned the loss of Joan's friendship and support. In the service I prayed to get an understanding of Jesus' love for me.

I Don't Feel Loved by God

I didn't feel particularly loved. Quite the contrary. I felt God was being unduly hard on me. Yet the Bible clearly stated God loved His creatures—including me. The psalmist David and others wrote expressively of God's love and kindness. If I believed in God's goodness and what He said about loving me, I had to choose to accept this regardless of feelings. Once more, my will had to overrule my emotions.

Personalizing another of the Apostle Paul's prayers brought clarity and focus:

> I pray that I, being rooted and established in love, may have power, together with all the Lord's people, to grasp how wide and long and high and deep is the love of Christ, and to know this love that surpasses knowledge—that I may be filled to the measure of all the fullness of God. Now to him who is able to do immeasurably more than all I ask or imagine, according to his power that is at work within me, to him be glory . . . [65]

It seemed like all hell broke loose after I prayed this prayer. The battle intensified, and my journal records my questioning. The old struggle of equating behavioral problems with spiritual deficiencies rose up again:

> I've been having a hard time dealing with the demands of the heavy load I'm carrying at work. My reserves are getting dangerously low, as evidenced by the usual signs: teary, uptight, negative, irritable, fearful, supersensitive. I feel guilty about behaving that way, knowing full well this is not what the Lord wants of me, nor is this an example of "victorious Christian living." I get down on myself for not coping as I feel I should. I pray for God's strength and help, yet while I manage to

get through each day, I still seem to be drawing on diminishing reserves.

I don't believe this is a spiritual problem in the sense of my turning away from God. He is still the most important person in my life. Without Him I would not survive. I sense His presence through the Spirit, and the clearest indication that He is with me is the way He comes through in my moments of deepest need. When things get too much, He provides a way of escape or some relief.

However, in a sense, I think this is a spiritual problem. Why do I so easily slide into negative thinking and anticipating the worst? Having given up my deepest desire and dream of marriage, it seems I've swung in the opposite direction and almost expect that my life is going to continue to consist of living with a sense of loss and lack. I find it difficult to open myself to thinking that God would bless me with an enjoyable, fulfilling future. This makes no sense because my present circumstances are far beyond anything I ever thought they would be. I really do believe and have proved that God is a great compensator. He has been so gracious in His provision for my needs.

There seems to be something major missing in my thinking. I know intellectually that God loves me, cares for me, and promises to guide and provide for me. I don't understand why I have such a hard time accepting the love of Jesus on an emotional level. What am I doing wrong, or what should I be doing? Perhaps it's because I've never really known deep, unconditional, personal love and devotion. Maybe that's why I can't comprehend what it is like to be on the receiving end of such love.

So to a large extent, it is a spiritual problem. I need to pray for the Lord to open my mind and heart to receive His love, and to experience His healing touch in this area of my life.

I had no idea that a significant meeting lay ahead.

POINTER: Encountering "Giants" Along the Way is Inevitable, Overcoming them is Optional.

- Can you identify what "giants" block your path or impede your progress?

- What steps, if any, have you taken to overcome them?

POINTER REFLECTIONS:

25

"THE GREATEST COUNSELOR"

I will praise the LORD, who counsels me.

Psalm 16:7 (TNIV)

I cannot think of a better illustration of what I was about to experience than the story of Charlie Steinmetz and Henry Ford.

Steinmetz was physically handicapped but had one of the greatest minds in the field of electricity the world has ever known. He built the great generators for Henry Ford in his first plant in Dearborn, Michigan.

One day those generators broke down, and the plant came to a halt. They brought in ordinary mechanics and helpers who couldn't get the machinery going again. They were losing money. Then Ford called Steinmetz. The genius came, seemed to merely putter around for a few hours, and then threw the switch that put the great Ford plant back into operation.

A few days later Henry Ford received a bill from Steinmetz for $10,000. Although Ford was a very rich man, he returned the bill with a note, "Charlie, isn't this bill just a little high for a few hours of tinkering around on those motors?"

Steinmetz returned the bill to Ford. This time it read: "For tinkering around on the motors: $10. For knowing where to tinker: $9,990. Total: $10,000." Henry Ford paid the bill.

I was about to meet a tinkerer far more brilliant than Charlie Steinmetz—the Divine manufacturer's chosen emissary!

An Offer of Help

I had determined to seek emotional healing with the same fervor others seek physical healing, so I opened my mind to explore anything on the subject. My periodic bookstore browsing led me to *The Greatest Counselor in the World* by Lloyd John Ogilvie, former Chaplain of the United States Senate. I knew Dr. Ogilvie's writing exuded hope for change and authentic Christian living. He got my attention in the first few pages:

> We need someone to listen and understand—someone who will allow us to talk until we know what we are trying to say. And we need someone who will probe to the nub of the issue, who has the authority and wisdom to help us see any confusion in our thinking or distortions in our emotions. This someone not only needs

to lead us to the truth about ourselves and our lives, but also must possess the strength to empower us to act on what we know we must do and be. Above all, we need someone who has the power to heal our painful memories, sharpen our vision of what is best for our future, and catch us up in a purpose beyond ourselves—one that's big enough to fire our imaginations and give ultimate meaning and lasting joy to daily living.

That's a tall order. No friend, psychiatrist, psychologist, pastor, or spiritual advisor can meet all of these qualifications. But they may help lead us to the One Who has all these gifts. He alone has the omniscience, omnipresence, and omnipotence to be the kind of counselor we need. He can help us with our problems, relationships, and decisions for He knows everything. He is with us always, for He never sleeps. He has all power to give us strength and courage, for He is the Holy Spirit with us and wants to live within us."[*]

I began praying specifically that the Greatest Counselor would teach me how to achieve a healthy view of *Self*. The Counselor heard and began his tinkering.

To my astonishment, when I spent time in silent listening prayer, like Ogilvie, I gained amazing in-

---

[*]Lloyd John Ogilvie, *The Greatest Counselor in the World*, Ventura, CA: Regal Books, 1994, pp. 15, 16. Used by permission.

sights far beyond my own understanding. When I asked for help with stressful situations or strained relationships, often I was shown my part in causing the problem. Further, I received a revelation of what I should do or say to bring about healing.

A new dimension entered my life. Circumstances and relationships remained stormy, but I became aware of the stabilizing influence of the Spirit.

I recalled the days of my early sea voyages, especially those trips around the tempestuous Cape of Good Hope. The ship rolled and pitched. Furniture in the public areas not chained to the floor slid across the room. People lurched from side to side as they attempted to make their way down corridors. Taking a shower presented a challenge as the water either sprayed onto one wall or the other. It wasn't safe to venture out on the slippery, rolling decks, and anyone who did so ran the risk of injury, or worse, being flung overboard.

And then came stabilizers! More and more ships were fitted with these wonderful inventions. At the first sign of a rolling sea, the stabilizers unwind from the hull of the ship like fins on a fish, and calm is restored. So effective are they that on recent cruises I've begun to wonder if I was indeed on a ship. I would have liked just a little bit more "roll."

The Spirit became my "stabilizer." As soon as I hit turbulence, I learned to turn to God's Spirit for calm and comfort. Sometimes, as in real voyages, the seas continued to churn, but the effect of the stabilizing presence of the Spirit was real. Instead of bouncing around like a cork and being buffeted by waves, I now plowed steadily through the heavy seas.

An astounding truth lit up my mind—the intensely personal basis of the Spirit's dealings with me. He knows me intimately—past, present, and future. He comes to me in ways I never would have imagined. And he comes just when I'm ready to hear.

Another Jewel of Illumination

Confusion over the term "faith" still lingered. Time and again I heard Dad's voice, "Move forward in faith…" "Claim healing by faith." Jesus' words were often quoted, "If you believe, you will receive whatever you ask for in prayer."[66] I absorbed the message that the degree and level of my faith prompted God's actions. The interpretation of faith adopted by my grandparents and handed down by my parents had laid the groundwork for my "get from God" thinking and formed the basis for my praying to win the sweepstakes.

What I found so puzzling was the solid truth embedded in the erroneous application. Faith is God's foundational requirement; it is impossible to please Him without it. The difficulty arises over the varied definitions of "faith." According to Oswald Chambers:

> When faith overrides common sense, it becomes fanaticism. Common sense in opposition to faith becomes rationalism. The life of faith brings the two into a right relation. Common sense is not faith, and faith is not common sense; they stand in

the relation of the natural and the spiritual; of impulse and inspiration. [. . .] To turn head faith into a personal possession is a fight always, not sometimes. [. . .] Faith is the whole man rightly related to God by the power of the Spirit of Jesus Christ.*

Chambers' definition of faith opened my mind to the concept of *being* as opposed to *doing*. If I have accepted that Jesus Christ provided reconciliation with God, by faith I have moved into right relationship with Him and am in a state of "being."

It dawned on me where the root of my confusion lay. I had been taught that only the Pentecostals had the full understanding of what God made available to believers; the other denominations had a dead and formal brand of religion. As Grandma Connie wrote so long ago, the missionaries brought to them "light and revelation from the scriptures." The emphasis shifted from the core beliefs of Christianity to the expression of "spiritual gifts." *All* believers were encouraged to seek after *all* the gifts, be it faith, speaking in tongues, healing, or any other. This raised the bar, and an individual's level of spirituality became tied to the demonstration of one, two, or more of the gifts of the Spirit. As a consequence, I lived most of my life with a feeling

---

*Taken from *My Utmost for His Highest* by Oswald Chambers, © 1935 by Dodd Mead & Co., renewed © 1963 by the Oswald Chambers Publications Assn., Ltd. Used by permission of Discovery House Publishers, Grand Rapids, MI 49501. All rights reserved.

of spiritual inferiority. Certainly, I was unable to accept and enjoy being a child of God—I fell so far short of expectations.

The application of faith taught and practiced by my grandparents and parents did not refer to faith to trust in God but rather referred to the "gift of faith," given by the Spirit as he chooses.[67] Dad was given the "gift of faith"—faith to believe God to accomplish whatever extraordinary task He called him to do. This distinction put into focus an area that had been blurred for most of my life.

I kept reading. I kept praying. I tried to apply the lessons. But something blocked my understanding.

My search led me to a prayer in Ephesians 1:17 which I personalized:

> May the God of my Lord Jesus Christ, the glorious Father, give me the Spirit of wisdom and revelation, so that I may know him better. I pray also that *the eyes of my heart may be enlightened* in order that I may know the hope to which he has called me, the riches of his glorious inheritance in the saints, and his incomparably great power for us who believe (italics mine).

The thick fog that enveloped me so many years ago still enshrouded my mind. I needed the Spirit of revelation; I needed the eyes of my heart enlightened. This became my fervent daily prayer.

An Impossible Standard

I continued to ponder what I had read about the Biblical counseling approach to Christian living.

Warning lights flashed as I read Adams' conviction that only Biblical counselors know what a counselee should become as the result of counseling: he should look more like Christ.

There is a subtle message conveyed in Christian circles that places expectations on other Christians in the name of "discipleship" or "accountability." Well-meaning preachers, radio speakers, authors, church members, and friends exhorted me to: "Adjust your attitude!" "Become more like Jesus." "Learn to respond instead of react." "Walk in the Spirit and not in the 'flesh' (my own unspiritual desires and wants)." It seemed if I did all of the above, plus more, then I would find rest, contentment, and inner peace. I would also be a shining example of a true Christian.

In reality, this made me feel as though I were constantly being held up against the standard of the sinless, perfect God-Man. To nobody's surprise, least of all my own, I always came up short! And some well-intentioned Christian was frequently at hand, ready to point out where and how far I had missed the mark. While I redoubled my efforts on striving to get my behavioral self up to the spiritual standards I believed were expected of me, it was a lost cause, resulting in frustration and a deep sense of inadequacy as a Christian.

This "performance" thinking tied in to the doctrine of eternal security. If I could lose my salvation by sinning, then I had better behave according to my understanding of God's expectations. Such a belief had the effect of undermining any sense of security in God's love and grace. It placed me on the religious performance treadmill of constant effort, trying to please God to keep His approval and receive His blessings, while at the same time furtively looking around to gauge from others whether I was measuring up and "looking like Jesus."

Initiator of Change: The Counselor, Me, or the Spirit?

The meaning that came across to me from the proponents of "Biblical counseling" was that through mental discipline and application of scripture, as guided by a qualified, knowledgeable, Biblical counselor, I could shape myself into what and who God wanted me to be. If I properly interpreted scripture and applied it to my emotional difficulties, I would begin to change my thinking and act in a Christ-like manner.

I struggled with this teaching. It placed enormous emphasis on the importance of personal mental discipline in bringing about changes in behavior. It again seemed to emphasize that I am saved by God's grace (spiritual), but then I work very hard at applying scripture to change my behavior. The teaching centered on human effort. I was reminded of the six hundred-odd rules the Pharisees observed in Jesus' day as they endeavored to live up to what they believed were God's requirements. Nouthetic counselors concurred that change came from the heart, but the subtext message was that the avenue of that change was through the mind—application of scripture. While they tagged on the reminder to ask the Spirit's help in accomplishing these goals, this ran contrary to what I was beginning to understand about the role of the Spirit.

In *The Subtle Power of Spiritual Abuse*, David Johnson and Jeff VanVonderen outline the frightening implications of untrained, unqualified pastors, "fellow believers," and "elders" offering "Biblical counseling" to members of the congregation and those in need. These people are well meaning, they are sincere, many of them are godly. But inappropriately applying scripture to certain problem situations can cause untold emotional and spiritual damage. It is potentially explosive. More disturbing is the potential for legalism in the organized church, one person holding another up to a predetermined and individually interpreted standard.

I prayed, I read. Gently, the Greatest Counselor reminded me that Jesus did not introduce a new textbook on religion, the ultimate manual of "How To." He offered to change hearts. The transformation came from within and worked its way outward, not the other way around.

Like the gradual brightening of the sky as darkness gives way to dawn, light began to penetrate the fog in my mind. I was on the verge of grasping the most crucial step in understanding the Christian life—God's bountiful, abundant grace and all that He made available through Jesus. I am the recipient and beneficiary of His unmerited favor. God did not place performance expectations on me; I did this to myself by listening to the tapes of past programming and the misinterpretations of some Christians.

All the good behavior in the world will not grant me forgiveness from God. All the striving I can produce will not earn me any more favor than His abundant grace has already provided. My efforts to live the Christian life merely by reading and applying scripture are doomed to futility, frustration, and failure.

Stepping Off the Treadmill

Regrettably, my performance-driven behavior continued to get in the way. I tried to generate feelings of God's love. I asked for God's *help* in experiencing His love, whereas I should have been resting in the assurance that what He said was true. I needed to back off on my efforts and allow Him to do His work in me. For "it is God Who is all the while effectually at work in you— energizing and creating in you the power and desire— both to will and to work for His good pleasure, and satisfaction and delight."[68] My responsibility is to keep my will positioned to allow the Spirit to work in me. It's an "open hands" approach.

I added a new phrase to my daily prayer: "May your power continue to work in me to will and to act according to your good pleasure and purpose." This was a quantum leap forward in the reprogramming of my thinking. God could do in me what I could not do myself!

The Spirit is a master tinkerer.

POINTER: We Have Company on the Journey— A Helper

God is not a celestial torturer, constantly raising the bar of performance expectations. He never intended, nor desired, that we handle the challenges of life on our own. Jesus came to Earth not only to provide reconciliation to a holy God, but in order to understand what it was like to be human. His experiences with his disciples showed him how desperately humans need help in becoming what the Father designed them to be. When Jesus left, he sent the Spirit, the Helper, to take over the job.

- Imagine you are sitting across from "The Greatest Counselor." What would you like to unload?

- What has kept you spiritually, mentally, or emotionally trapped?

- What would you like to change? Ask "The Helper" to do in you what you have found you cannot do for yourself.

POINTER REFLECTIONS:

26

TRAINING ... AND MORE TRAINING

Whatever the struggle continue the climb
it may be only one step to the summit.

—Diane Westlake

New Year's Eve 2001. I sat with friends at dinner and listened as they talked about goals and resolutions for the New Year. I had none—and had no interest in setting any. I only wanted to survive and hope for a better year ahead. Events of the past few months had left me feeling like a wrung-out rag. The effects of my Wisdom School lessons were overshadowed by demands at work as deadlines approached. I ran on empty, as if I had a leaky big toe where all my energy seeped out. I prayed daily for the strength, wisdom, insight, and understanding I needed for my many responsibilities. I wanted to respond to the challenges in a Christ-like manner.

To my utter dismay, a message from the Greatest Counselor insistently clamored at the edges of my mind, "It's time to move on." I didn't want to hear this. I hate job changes and had decided after the last one to stay put until I eventually retired. The mere thought of having to look for another job sent me into an instant emotional decline. The economy was unstable. My earnings in 2000 had been the best yet, and I enjoyed having discretionary money. It had taken me eight years to climb out of the financial hole left by my early retirement from Delta.

I stifled the inner voice. It made no sense to consider again giving up a good income and security. I would try harder to make it work, take better care of my health and pace myself.

But the Spirit didn't give up. I came to the inescapable conclusion I was temperamentally unsuited to my current push and drive environment. It would never be a good fit. The Greatest Counselor apparently had other plans in mind. He was far more interested in completing my healing than seeing I had a good income.

Decision Time

In my mind, I stood at a fork in the road. One route pointed to a familiar path where my emotions ruled and dictated behavior. I knew from past experience that my feet could be sucked into the quicksand that lurked under seemingly secure rocks and leaves. Pitfalls and hazards lay everywhere.

The second route led up the side of a steep mountain slope. The frighteningly narrow path was barely evident in places. Giant boulders blocked the way. Unimaginable scary beasts hid in the grasses and bushes on either side of the road—but the path led upward, away from the swamps, disappearing into the blue sky of the horizon.

My will gave me freedom to choose my route. The familiar path would prolong the "bump along the bottom" pattern of the past. The unfamiliar path looked treacherous. Walking there would require discipline and effort. But the promise of freedom beckoned, holding out hope for better days ahead.

The Greatest Counselor urged me to take my newfound knowledge and begin connecting the dots. My will kicked in and overruled the downward pull of emotions. I chose the upward route—a deliberate, conscious decision. I would begin the arduous climb.

A sense of peace came over me when I turned in my resignation, even though I faced an uncertain future. I planned to take several weeks off, then no doubt the Lord would open the next door of opportunity, and I'd be off and running once more. Perhaps I could go into business for myself?

At first, freedom from work restrictions made me agitated and restless. I prowled around doing odd jobs. Warm weather lured me outdoors, and I again watched the reawakening of life in my garden. Someone told me when I first arrived in Atlanta that once I had experienced spring in the area I would never want to leave. Well, that really wasn't why I stayed, but each year the beauty that emerged after the deadness of winter lifted my spirit.

No fixed schedule meant I could spend as long as I wanted reading scriptures, devotionals, other books, or listening to tapes. Gently, God's Spirit ministered to my heart and mind, restoring my soul.

This Course is Hard!

My self-prescribed period of rest came to an end. No matter how I procrastinated, the despised job-hunting chore loomed ahead. Conventional wisdom urged me to network, so I talked to contacts. Nothing materialized. I responded to job ads. Despite my stellar qualifications for any administrative position, there was no flood of phone calls from people dying for my services. Life got slower and slower. Each day I slipped into greater isolation and obscurity.

Jacque, my encourager, read a comment from one of her daily devotionals that shed light on what might be happening. It pointed out that when God drastically slows our pace along life's road, it could be because we're about to face a hairpin bend. If we don't slow down, we could wreck ourselves.

The feeling that I was headed in a new, unknown direction intensified. A pertinent scripture offered encouragement: "I will lead the blind by ways they have not known, along unfamiliar paths I will guide them; I will turn the darkness into light before them and make the rough places smooth. These are the things I will do; I will not forsake them."[69]

What an apt analogy. I inched along like a blind person being led down an unfamiliar path, one teeny step after another. At times strangling fear gripped me, and I could not shake the feeling of heading straight for a cliff. Calmly, the Spirit reminded me who was leading and what He had promised. No matter what lay ahead on the path, He would not forsake or abandon me. I drew courage from this thought.

I had landed in a graduate level Skill for Living course, taught by the Master Teacher, Jesus, with counseling by the Greatest Counselor, the Spirit. The course material had been notched up, and the lessons intensified.

A longing started small and grew within me. The Divine Lover was calling, and I wanted to follow. My mundane life needed a touch of heroism. Up to this point, I had seen myself as one of many, struggling along the Christian path. Now I could almost feel Jesus' arm go around my shoulders and hear him as he turned to me and said: "Joy, will you come with me? Will you trust me on this new adventure?" It became intensely personal.

"Yes, Lord, I'll go with you," I whispered. "I want to learn to fully trust you and to live the free and abundant life you promised."

It's a good thing the future is veiled from us. Had I known what lay ahead, I would have crumpled into a pathetic, quivering mass.

Learning Raw Trust in an Invisible God

Weeks passed with no sign of a job. I wanted an adventure, but this was nerve-wracking. It bordered on a disaster. I had a home to maintain and needed an income. My savings dwindled with each month's bills. I sent out another batch of résumés—to no avail. No responses and no leads.

One of my character traits is an overwhelming sense of responsibility. It may be as a result of being the elder child, or my parents programmed it into me when they gave me responsibilities at too early an age. I assumed the weight of the well-being of my parents, the well-being of extended family members, the well-being of friends, and the well-being of the whole ungodly world. Being single and solely responsible for my future weighed heavily and added to my panic.

"I have no safety net," I wailed to Jacque in a fit of despondency. "I'm all alone! I've got no one. I have no hope of a rich uncle leaving me an inheritance. I don't even have a family to fall back on." The pity party was going full swing that day.

"Joy, you do have a safety net. The Lord is your safety net!" she wisely responded.

I was reminded of the story of the man who fell over the side of a cliff. Arms flailing, he grabbed a tree branch on his way down and clung precariously to it.

"Help!" he shouted. "Is anybody down there?"

"Yes," came a strong voice. "I'm here; I'll help you."

"Can you come up here and get me?"

"No, just let go, I'll catch you," was the response.

The man was silent for a while as he considered this option. Then he made his decision.

"Is anybody else down there?" he called.

As someone prone to fear, letting go of the branch and trusting I would not crash was the most terrifying step I could take. My heart wanted to respond in simple, childlike faith in a good God; my mind and emotions reared up in alarm at being so foolhardy. This path was going in a decidedly uncomfortable direction, totally contrary to the way I wanted.

For years I had unwaveringly encouraged others to trust God with whatever problems they faced. Like Dad, I adopted a "Don't worry, dear, the Lord will sort it out" approach. It came as a shock to discover my confidence was always strongest when it applied to others' lives. I could speak with assurance about a good God and His promises as long as my basic needs were being met. All my resolute affirmations of faith and trust evaporated when the walls of my little security house showed signs of cracking.

Now, dark storm clouds filled the horizon of my future as my typical thought pattern seized hold. Inescapable poverty loomed ahead; ill health would surely follow. I would no doubt have to sell my lovely home and move into some tenement type accommodations. There would be nobody to look after me as I painfully eked out my days until, with a sigh of relief, I died and was buried somewhere. Everything I knew intellectually about God and His proven track record of faithfulness in my life to this point became erased like writing on a chalkboard. I was immobilized by fear.

A Lifeline from the Grocery Store

On one of my grocery store jaunts I scanned a book display. A title leapt out at me: *100 Ways to Obtain Peace— Overcoming Anxiety.* I grabbed it like a drowning person reaching for a lifeline. What a great find! A treasure of pithy spiritual and practical encouragement fell into my hands.

We are prone to a terrible habit: we want to be able to figure everything out and have events happen according to our plans. When things go awry, we become confused and disturbed. Whenever our needs are involved, our tendency to worry and fret increases. Instead of being crushed, we should be challenged. The challenge is to rely on Jesus to meet those needs. He promises to take care of us and provide for us. Take the challenge, and let that bad habit die. Stop figuring and start "faithing"![70]

The authors were mind readers. I am always trying to figure out the future. Whenever I found my anxiety level rising I quoted out loud, "Stop figuring and start 'faithing.'"

I placed this affirmation note next to my make-up mirror where I couldn't miss it.

Whose Voice Are You Listening To?

Gently, but firmly, the Master Teacher introduced more course material. Prior questions relating to God, Jesus, and the role of the Spirit were settled, but I remained extremely wobbly on issues relating to my deepest needs. Satan, the Deceiver, pushed me around because I lacked the mental fortitude to stand him down. At the first insidious whisper of doubt, "Did God really say . . . ?" my knees buckled, and I slumped into a quagmire of doubt, my mind filled with Satan's "How do you know that God is going to meet your needs? Maybe you made a mistake in leaving your good job. After all, God directed you to that job in the first place."

I discovered the most difficult aspect of resisting temptation is recognizing it. It is virtually impossible to identify the source of the voices I "hear" in my mind without clear guidelines. How do I know what I am hearing is not a throw-over from past programming? How can I tell if the communication is from God when it appears to go against human reasoning? How can I filter out Satan's devious messages?

Jesus is Truth; Satan the master deceiver. Satan is not omniscient, all-knowing. He does not read our thoughts in advance nor can he know our hearts like God does. Yet he understands human nature well enough to strike where we are most vulnerable. Satan does not tempt me with something I can easily resist. He's much cleverer. His temptations are always reasonable, logical, appealing, and often disguised in pious terms. He employs anything and anyone to distract me. His primary goal is to deflect the truth of what God wants me to learn. Identifying the source of what pops into my mind presents a huge challenge.

> **Jesus:** "Trust me. I have it all under control. My plan for you is unfolding right on schedule."
> **Satan:** "How do you know it's not your emotions talking? You know they are unpredictable and unstable."
> **Friends:** "God has given you abilities. You need an income. The solution is to get out there and find a job."

> **The Holy Spirit:** "Relax. What's more important right now? Learning lessons that will carry you through the rest of your life or earning a salary? You wanted emotional healing. This is the way to it."

My Mom, Claudia, and I developed a means of communicating with each other in crowded or somewhat distant places. We called "Yoo-hoo" at a certain pitch and volume. Instantly, the others recognized the voice and traced the location of the caller.

This is obviously what Jesus meant when he spoke about himself as the Good Shepherd, "He calls his own sheep by name and leads them out. When he has brought out all his own, he goes on ahead of them, and his sheep follow him because they know his voice."[71]

The secret lay in learning to recognize the voice behind the message. God calls me to be more than I am. Satan sows doubt in my mind. He appeals to logic, reason, need, desire, the same approach he used with Jesus when he met him in the wilderness. Jesus showed the only way to combat Satan's deception is countering with the truth of scripture. Once God's word is programmed into my thinking, the Spirit surfaces the instruction I need in times of testing.

Still, how can I be sure that what I am hearing truly comes from God? I can't in myself. But I have learned to run to scripture to see if it lines up with God's commands and the teachings of Jesus. I revert to my prayer, "Lord Jesus, you are Truth. Please reveal truth to me in this situation."

If what I am hearing and feeling does line up with God's word, if I believe I am being led in a certain direction and no red warning lights flash in my mind, all I can do is trust that the Spirit will not allow me to go astray. Trust that if I somehow misinterpret the message, the Spirit will throw up a roadblock and save me in time to prevent serious damage. Wise counsel from trusted Christian friends is also a vital element.

It takes practice, and it takes time. Like any skill, it is honed through use. But I do not know of anything so freeing as learning how to listen and identify the voice of the Spirit—and then trusting that voice implicitly. It is inexplicable. Its amazing reality has to be experienced to be appreciated.

Slowly, almost imperceptibly at first, I became calmer. The image of resting, listening, and learning at the feet of the Master gave meaning to the seeming confusion of my days.

A revolutionary concept formed in my mind. Instead of allowing a negative perception of my circumstances to feed my fears, I could view this positively, as an investment in my mental, physical, emotional, and spiritual health—my future. I could regard the funds for my expenses as tuition costs in God's graduate school.

I sought strength in my little book.

> We don't get enough rest—spiritual rest, that is. The routine panic in which many of us live daily is indicative of the inner merry-go-round that spins even faster. Whenever pressure points come . . . we churn away on the inside like an electric ice-cream maker.

It's hard work to learn how to rest properly. We believe we are remiss to just sit quietly at the feet of Jesus. [. . .] Resting spiritually is not laziness. It does not mean shirking responsibility. It is the calm assurance that God is working right on schedule.[72]

I placed another affirmation note in front of one of my most precious possessions—my coffeemaker: "Relax Joy! Jesus has everything under control."

The note became wrinkled and stained, but its message calmed my fears and restored my perspective.

Rerecording the Tapes

Psychologists say it takes about twenty-one days to change thinking. I knew from experience that merely reading scripture or helpful comments in a book did not effect a lasting change. I had to rerecord the tapes in my head.

To do this, I plastered more notes around the house that I could see every day. My home began to look like the inside of the tree in the Post-It Notes™ commercial, where the squirrel posted reminders of where he hid the nuts.

I captioned this set of affirmation notes "Keeping Your Focus; Changing Your Thinking."

- Do you need it (the provision) now? When you need it, it will be there! God is trustworthy, He won't let you down. (Joan)
- You wanted to learn to live with reckless abandon based on total trust

in your loving Heavenly Father. Now's your chance—don't blow it!

- You committed to follow your Heavenly Lover on whatever adventure he chose to take you on. Why are you so scared? Why are you letting fear from your past and your natural negative thinking override what you know in your heart to be true? God's way is perfect, His timing is perfect, and He will come through in the nick of time with exactly the right provision.

- God keeps His promises! He is not a man that He should lie, nor a son of man that He should change his mind. He does not speak and not act; He does not promise and not fulfill.[73] He has promised to guide, provide for, strengthen, and be with you every step of the way. Focus on this!

- You are not on poverty row—you have sufficient money to cover your expenses for a while. Rest and wait to see what door opens.

- As best you know how, you are endeavoring to put God first, to acknowledge Him, trust Him, enjoy His presence and His provision. You can therefore expect Him to honor His commitment to keep His word.

- The sovereign ruler of the universe (*El Elyon*) is acting on your behalf even as you write this. Change your thinking from passivity and fearfulness to joyous expectation of what God is going to do.

- You are not God's office manager! You do not need to come up with a solution to this situation.
- God delights in His name and His word. His reputation is on the line, not yours.

Reprogramming takes work—and time. It is a daily exercise in mental discipline.

POINTER: Expect Nerve-wracking Circumstances

There comes a point along the "trust" journey when God ups the ante. The only way to ride out such circumstances is to keep your will solidly, firmly positioned on the support column of the character of God. Then trust the Spirit to keep you on course.

- Do you see any parallel in your own situation to what I experienced?

- Are you facing inexplicable challenges?

- Is your mind filled with confusing messages?

- Why not ask God's Spirit to help you sift through them to determine what he may be trying to say to you, or teach you?

God has a way of leading us in directions that defy conventional wisdom.

POINTER REFLECTIONS:

27
THE ULTIMATE CRISIS

*Will the clay say to the potter, 'What are you doing?'
Or the thing you are making say, 'He has no hands?'*

Isaiah 45:9 (NASB)

Instead of circumstances becoming easier and more understandable, the difficulties increased. I wanted God in my life, and I certainly wanted His blessings, protection, preservation, and provision. However, I also felt He owed me some compensation. One of my most hopeful scriptures was, "Then I will make up to you for the years that the swarming locust has eaten."[74]

The rub came when my preconceived notions of how God should do this conflicted with His. David Seamands described this dilemma:

Self-surrender is the ultimate crisis because it represents the ultimate spiritual battle. Everything else in Christian experience is a preamble to this. [. . .] All of these important steps are the growing pains through which God "leads His dear children along," until we finally see what the real challenge is. Everything up to this point has been a minor skirmish in comparison to the ultimate battle to which we are being led lovingly, ruthlessly, relentlessly, wooingly but oh, so firmly. We are being taken by the Holy Spirit to the place where we see that the real issue is the surrender of self to the lordship of Jesus Christ. [. . .] It is at the cross that the crucifixion of the self-centeredness of my ego is going to take place. And this is the greatest battle of every life.

The Holy Spirit takes us through this process of self-exposure so that we will see what the real issue is. For our basic sin lies much deeper than the daily sins which are its outward form [. . .] The real sin is the unsurrenderedness of the ego. This sin is the root; the sins are the fruit.[*]

The "Gentle Jesus" of Sunday School turns out to be a demanding leader. He warns us to count the cost before

---

[*]David A. Seamands, *Putting Away Childish Things,* Indianapolis, IN: Light and Life Communications, 1999, pp. 119-120. Used by permission.

signing up with him. Then he winnows and sifts his followers, separating the dabblers from the disciples.

I understood that willful disobedience (sin) separates us from God. I also understood that God's grace reaches over the dividing line to restore us to Him. What did Seamands mean by "the real sin is the unsurrenderedness of the ego?" I had heard preachers all my life quote the Apostle Paul's words in Galatians, "I have been crucified with Christ—[in Him] I have shared His crucifixion; it is no longer I who live, but Christ, the Messiah, lives in me; and the life I now live in the body I live by faith—by adherence to and reliance on and [complete] trust—in the Son of God, Who loved me and gave Himself up for me."[75]

Eugene Peterson interprets this scripture as "I tried keeping rules and working my head off to please God, and it didn't work; so I quit so that I could simply be, so I could live in harmony with God. Christ's life showed me how and enabled me to do it. I identified myself completely with him; indeed I have been crucified with Christ. My ego is no longer central."*

I now faced the ultimate crisis—the surrender of my ego, the core of my self-will.

"Bless You, Job"

The story of Job in the Old Testament has been the subject of countless sermons and featured in many books. People are inclined to think of Job primarily as an example of patience through intense suffering and loss. This is certainly true, and his quiet trust in the

---

*Eugene H. Peterson, *Traveling Light*, Colorado Springs, CO: Helmers & Howard, 1988, p. 72. Used by permission.

character of the God he knew and loved is evidenced by his unwillingness to follow his wife's advice to curse God and die. But as I pondered Job's plight and his reaction to circumstances, I developed a different perspective on the story.

Job was God's beloved child. He honored God, served Him faithfully, and tried his best to be obedient. He was a great father to his ten children, praying for them and offering sacrifices on their behalf. He taught them to worship the one true God and stay away from idols. Job did everything right. Yet without warning his circumstances took a dramatic downturn. Loss after loss inexplicably rained down upon him. His herds of oxen, donkeys, sheep, and camels, along with the responsible servants, were destroyed. The same day, his seven sons and three daughters were killed by a tornado-like wind which caused the house in which they were meeting to collapse. Later, Job was struck down with painful, festering sores.

Scripture gives us a glimpse into the drama being played out in heaven in Chapter 1 of the Book of Job, but at the time Job had no idea. Day after day he wrestled with his calamitous situation and tried to reconcile this with his concept of a loving God. Well-intentioned, kind friends offered their perspective—which was just that, their perspective. They spent their time speculating and offering advice to Job on how he should respond in order to "regain" God's favor. They, too, didn't have a clue what was going on. And Job kept thrashing around in his own mind for an answer to his predicament.

I find it significant that God never did answer Job's question, "Why?" Instead He gave Job a revelation of Himself—His might, power, and glory. He lets Job know in no uncertain terms that He is God, creator of the inanimate world (Job 38) and the animate world (Job 39). He is sovereign ruler over everything (Job 40).

Finally, Job humbly confesses, "My ears had heard of you but now my eyes have seen you. Therefore I despise myself and repent in dust and ashes."[76] He acknowledged the supremacy of God. Job faced the ultimate crisis—coming to the point of self-surrender, trusting without understanding.

There is no record God ever gave Job an explanation of the cosmic wager that prompted the calamities which came into his life. Yet I love the way the book ends, "After this, Job lived a hundred and forty years; he saw his children and their children to the fourth generation. And so he died, old and full of years."[77] The scars of his emotional pain must have stayed with him as memories of his first set of children flashed into his mind, yet God graciously blessed Job more in his later years than He had in his earlier years.

Hidden in the poetry of this magnificent story is a phrase that has profound meaning when viewed in the context of relationships. Job 42:15 reads, "Nowhere in all the land were there found women as beautiful as Job's daughters, and their father granted them an inheritance along with their brothers." This was unheard of in that patriarchal society. Only sons inherited. Job's encounter with God not only changed his conception of the Almighty, it changed his estimation of his relationships.

My own "why" reminded me of a spoiled, insistent child tugging at the skirt of her mother. I was as guilty of trying to get God to give me an explanation for my difficult circumstances as Job had been. It was futile to try to figure out and second-guess God's actions—or inaction. It was equally futile to think that anyone else—well-meaning friend, pastor, teacher, or counselor—could figure it out, either. There are times when circumstances are simply inexplicable.

So did I resign myself to a fatalistic view of life, accepting that I'm just a pawn on a giant chessboard? No! As someone said, "When you can't trace God's hand, trust His heart."

God used the same method with me as He did with Job. I didn't hear His audible voice, yet it was just as definite a message as if I had. He began to give me a greater revelation of Himself.

The Greatest Counselor orchestrated my participation in a class on Kay Arthur's devotional study, *Lord, I Want to Know You.* It blew the lid off my meager concept of God. I caught the significance of what He wanted to convey about His character when He revealed His names, and I understood in a new way the source of the life Jesus spoke about—the abundant life. Gone was my childish interpretation that centered on me and my needs. With insight and clarity I saw God's design.

A wave of abject contrition swept over me as I compared the majesty and power of God with the speck of dust demanding answers. God is God, and I'm not. He does as He pleases. In fact, he clearly warned me of this: "'For my thoughts are not your thoughts, neither are your ways my ways,' declares the Lord. 'As the heavens are higher than the earth, so are my ways higher than your ways and my thoughts than your thoughts.'"[78] But this time there was no hint of resignation—just total acceptance.

"Oh, God, forgive me," I prayed. "Forgive me for my arrogance in demanding answers to my circumstances. Help me to trust in your wisdom and your great heart of love. Help me to know that nothing comes my way unless it is filtered through your fingers of unfailing love. I accept that you know what you are doing even when I haven't a clue, and that you desire my ultimate good."

Bowing my will and surrendering my ego to the sovereignty and wisdom of God was like breaking through a cloud barrier into brilliant sunshine. There were things I still couldn't understand. But I had been given a glimpse into the great heart of God, and I would never be the same. I could trust that because He is who He is, He will do what is best for me.

The battle over surrender of the ego is monumental! The conflict is fierce. The Deceiver will do everything in his power to thwart progress. Yet, coming to the point of saying "OK, Lord, you're now in charge" is crucial for spiritual growth. As Joan so often told me, "Joy, He is trustworthy!"

POINTER: Self-surrender is the Ultimate Challenge

- Have there been situations in your life when you've asked God "Why?" only to have Him remain silent?

- If so, what were the circumstances?

- In such situations, we have two choices: rebel and get angry or submit and wait it out.

- Can you look back on times when you did one or the other?

- What were the results?

POINTER REFLECTIONS:

PART NINE

LIFE IN BALANCE

28

AN INTEGRATING FORCE

'Not by might, nor by power, but by My Spirit' says the LORD Almighty.

Zechariah 4:6 (TNIV)

The Bible records in honest detail how the Israelites experienced ongoing difficulties in learning to accept and trust the invisible God. After years of endless waiting, the order came to move forward under Joshua's leadership to the land God had promised would be theirs. Yahweh's guidance en route was clearly evident through numerous instances of gracious intervention. However, no sooner had the people settled in the Promised Land than they reverted to old patterns of thinking. They asked God to give them a king like all the nations around them. They said it was important to have a visible leader, someone they could look up to and show off to others. God was hurt by this patent rejection of His sole leadership and warned them of the potential dangers in having a monarch. They were insistent, and He acceded to their wish.

The history of the Israelites from then on seesaws through good king, bad king, God worship, idol worship. It took the drastic step of God allowing the entire nation to be taken captive by the Babylonians centuries later before the people got the Egyptian gods and idol worship out of their system. Undoing past programming doesn't come easy.

I've often smugly thought that if I were among the Israelites and had witnessed and experienced the same miraculous interventions of God, I wouldn't have a problem trusting Him. Or would I?

With the benefit of history and hindsight, I can trace God's plan as it unfolded over the centuries. I know the ups and downs of the Israelite nation. I know about the fulfillment of the prophecies concerning Jesus. I can read the record of his life on earth, his death and resurrection. I am the beneficiary of the presence of the Spirit in the world.

Yet, I must confess that my power struggle with an invisible God is as intense as anything the Israelites demonstrated. Like them, I want His blessings, protection, and provision, all on my terms and according to my timetable. When nothing happens and I get tired of waiting, my thoughts drift to creating something visible to fill my life—a relationship, career, new car, overseas trip, or more entertainment and indulgent pleasure. It's not that I want to replace God; I merely want something additional. I want to create my own little "golden calf." Idolatry is counting on something other than God.

Was an up and down existence, a fluctuating sense of God's involvement and presence to be my lot as well?

Back to the Model

My attention again turned to the equal-arm balance model. Intellectually, I grasped the overall concept and recognized the potential for balance built into the design. However, I had lived all my life with a disconnect between what my head told me and what my emotions did. I needed an integrating force. The last words uttered on earth by Dad clamored at my mind: "Not by might, nor by power, but by My Spirit . . ."

What if my equal-arm balance were animated? What if God's power could connect the four components: the support column, the crossbar of my will, and the two suspended pans of relationships with others and my relationship with myself?

I imagined Almighty God as the generator, or computer chip, and Jesus Christ as the conduit. The Spirit became the power charge flowing upwards and outwards, into my deepest recesses, and touching my relationships with others.

The crossbar of my will functioned as the dial that controlled the current. My free will granted me the prerogative to open the valve and allow the power to course through my being. Or, I could regulate its access as God and I shared control to a lesser or greater extent. It also gave me the option to switch off the flow.

I chose to turn the dial wide open, to allow the Spirit uninhibited access to work outwardly in my relationships with *Others* and inwardly in the healing of *Self.*

Power to Change Thinking

My mental discipline was like pins in a bowling alley. At the first well-aimed blow of the ball, they scattered. All my good intentions stood upright and secure until something raised a question in my mind, and then they were bowled over. I scrambled to gather up the pins of my resolve and purposed to be stronger next time—until the doubts reared themselves and down I went again.

The Master Teacher pointed out that such behavior was my choice, not the inevitable result of my emotional temperament. Blows in life are inescapable, but my response to the difficulties can change. I can't control the thoughts that pop into my head since they come from varying sources. But I can control the filter. I examine the thoughts and decide whether they linger in my mind, settle down and make a home, or whether they get thrown out.

The Apostle Paul reminded me that "For the Spirit God gave us does not make us timid, but gives us power, love and self-discipline."[79] He summed up our ammunition for the mental battle in his letter to the Corinthians, "The weapons we fight with are not the weapons of the world. On the contrary, they have divine power to demolish strongholds. We demolish arguments and every pretension that sets itself up against the knowledge of God, and *we take captive every thought to make it obedient to Christ*" (italics mine).[80]

Taking captive every thought is switching on the filtering system—and maintaining it. Maybe this is why Jesus told us to love God with *all our mind* as well as with all our heart.

A Vigorous Life Force

We are not mature individuals at twenty-h
we become mature Christian believers after se
Each is a lifetime process.

Psychologists have identified the stages of g
from infancy to the sunset of life. Healthy pe
commit to keep on growing, developing mind a
body through the span of their years. Spiritually health
people recognize that spiritual maturity is not injected
while we sleep. There is no spiritual plateau onto which
we climb and happily rest. Physical living and spiritual
living both call for discipline:

- Spiritual discipline—the commitment
to search for truth, the will to trust an
invisible God even when He seems dis-
tracted and distant, and the determination to learn and study God's word.
- Mental discipline—learning to filter
out negative thoughts and manage
emotions.
- Physical discipline—committing to
a regular exercise program, eating
moderately, getting sufficient sleep,
and building personal down time into
the schedule.
- Social discipline—establishing balance between wholesome activities
and those that infringe on time that
could be spent more profitably; seeking out "safe" people and avoiding
toxic relationships.

- Financial discipline—giving to God first, setting personal and family goals, and then learning contentment.

Recognizing there are stages in the spiritual growth process as there are in the physical realm helps me become more accepting of others' behavior. Reflecting on my own bumpy path motivates me to show compassion and offer encouragement to those who may be a few steps behind.

Becoming a Christian did not instantly transform me into a saintly, angelic-type being. My eternal destiny was redirected, my personality invited to participate in the lifetime process of becoming conformed to the image of Christ, but my real self didn't change. Christian behavior becomes an expression of individual background, temperament, theological knowledge—or lack thereof—and emotional makeup. Any subject open to human interpretation can be misinterpreted. I have learned to expect the unexpected and unpredictable when tapping into emotions.

Drawing from the Power Source

Sometimes I simply get weary of the battle. The process is too long, too confusing, too exhausting. That's when the support, prayers, and encouragement of trusted friends who are believers is invaluable, especially from those individuals who are clearly in the same struggle to overcome the effects of their past.

The importance of embedding God's Word into my thinking cannot be overemphasized. It's like rerecording old tapes. I have to put new thoughts and messages into my mind based on God's view of me, not on past programming.

Daily prayer time has now become a habit. Lloyd John Ogilvie's *Conversation with God* presents the view that prayer is simply that, conversation with God— reflecting on who He is, confessing shortcomings, interceding for others, presenting requests and needs, drawing strength from the Spirit. Ogilvie's daily devotionals, *God's Best for My Life* and *God's Strength for This Day* keep my wayward thoughts pointed in the right direction. In my quiet time, I position myself once more at the base of the fountain of an overflowing God, to be drenched in His goodness, love, and grace.

Regular sessions with the Greatest Counselor are my "stabilizers." When storms come and circumstances pile up on me, I withdraw into total silence and solitude, pour out my anxieties and hurts to my Counselor, and allow the Spirit to do in me what I cannot do for myself. Sometimes he gives a new perspective on the situation, or a soothing calm comes over my troubled soul. Most times I am directed back to a pertinent scripture which infuses strength.

I do believe in the counsel contained in the Bible. I simply found that it works like rehabilitation after surgery. The root problem, like a broken bone or a tumor, has to be tackled first.

Strength for the Battle

I again wished that God would unzip my head, remove my brain, and insert a new memory, like an upgrade on my computer. Yet His dealings with the Israelites revealed that is generally not His way.

Idol-worshipping pagans inhabited the homeland God promised to give His people. It is curious that an all-powerful, transcendent Yahweh who had miraculously engineered the release from slavery of His people elected not to wipe out the idol-worshippers. Instead, He trained His people to fight. He promised to be with them in the battle, not to spare them from the battle.

Yahweh was explicit in His instructions to utterly destroy the inhabitants of the territory, to clear them out. Such a harsh, rigid stance would draw an avalanche of criticism in our modern politically correct society, yet God knew the hearts of the people. He had instructed them to have no other gods before Him, and He foresaw the potential for straying from this purpose if the people tried to coexist with the idol-worshippers. God wanted nothing to stand in the way of the relationship He desired to build and maintain with the Israelites. Consequently, the Israelites understood they had to remove the "giants" in the land before they could fully enjoy their new possession and the accompanying blessings.

One by one I had been felling my own "giants" as I doggedly dealt with the issues of my past. The battle was fierce and exhausting. I'd get one down, and three more popped out unexpectedly from behind the bushes. They seemed to lurk everywhere, ready to blindside me at any time. When I thought I'd dealt with them all, one more leaped out brandishing the sword of hurt and pain. Sometimes I let out a mental "rebel yell," and drawing on the power in Jesus' name, told them to back off and leave me alone. But there were times when I felt too tired to even try. Feebly, I groped for a firmer grip on my sword in order to fend off the blows.

The Apostle Paul offers hope for such times. He tells me that when I can no longer fight, I am to simply stand.

> Finally, be strong in the Lord and in his mighty power. Put on the full armor of God so that you can take your stand against the devil's schemes. [...] Therefore put on the full armor of God, so that when the day of evil comes, you may be able to stand your ground, and after you have done everything, to stand.[81]

I thought again of the words of "A Firm Foundation," which had offered such comfort and support after Mom's death:

> Fear not, I am with thee, O be not dismayed.
> I, I am thy God and will still give thee aid:
> I'll strengthen thee, help thee, and cause thee to stand, *Upheld by My righteous, omnipotent hand.*" (emphasis and italics mine)[82]

Victories are hard won; they are not handed out like party favors. I have found that all hell breaks loose when Satan believes I am on the point of learning a major spiritual lesson or breaking free of the fears that debilitate me. He hurls his entire arsenal of doubts, lies, distortions, allurements, temptations, and twisted truth at me in an attempt to keep me in bondage, or at the very least, to impede progress.

When my armor slips and Satan's arrows pierce and it seems the battle is going the wrong way, an all-powerful hand reaches down to grasp mine. He picks me up, dusts me off, replaces the sword, straightens the armor, and offers cold water to refresh. Strength flows like an electric current into my weakened frame and wilting spirit. I am revived, I regain perspective, and I am encouraged to stay in the battle until the victory is won. And by God's strength, I know I will win in the end.

Proverbs 4:18 sums it up, ". . . the path of the righteous is like the light of dawn, that shines brighter and brighter until the full day" (NASB).

It's a process, and it takes a lifetime.

Power to Become a Super Conqueror

A conqueror in ancient times was one who overcame the enemy. A super conqueror was one who not only overcame the enemy but also made the conquered serve his purposes. It was one thing to beat a king in battle and have him spend his life under house arrest in a distant village. It was quite another to have that king serve the conqueror in some capacity on a daily basis. The latter demonstrated to everyone the unquestioned, overwhelming nature of the victory.

As rays of light penetrated the fog in my mind, I found a new dream forming. I wanted to be a super conqueror. I wanted to not only overcome the issues and problems of my past, but to so completely rise above them that they would become my servants in the future.

Romans 8 tells me that ". . . we know that in all things God works for the good of those who love him, who have been called according to his purpose. [. . .] If God is for us, who can be against us? [. . .] Who shall separate us from the love of Christ? Shall trouble or hardship or persecution or famine or nakedness or danger or sword? [. . .] No, in all these things (*neglect, loss, deprivation, confusion, error*) we are more than conquerors through him who loved us" (italics mine).[83]

By the power of God working in me, I can become a Super Conqueror.

My crossbar is liable to buckle on occasion, tilt precariously, even collapse. Ongoing adjustments in the placement and operation of my will are inherent in the design. It is a learning process. My great consolation comes from the knowledge that God Himself works with my will to see my crossbar never falls off.

A tremendous power supply and amazing resources are available to me. I choose by my will to open my heart and mind to believe, and receive.

> Now to Him Who, by (in consequence of) the [action of His] power that is at work within us, is able to [carry out His purpose and] do superabundantly, far over and above all that we [dare] ask or think—infinitely beyond our highest prayers, desires, thoughts, hopes or dreams—to Him be glory in the church and in Christ Jesus throughout all generations, for ever and ever.[84]

POINTER: Connect to the Power Source

- Think about how God can help you, individually, through the process of learning to live life to the fullest.

- What would life be like for you if you aspired to the status of Super Conqueror?

- Your will is key in the whole process. Are you willing to let God begin working in you?

- Open the dial of your will to allow the flow of God's power into your heart and mind—and watch what happens! He gives courage to overcome the past, infuses strength for the present, and holds out bright hope for the future.

POINTER REFLECTIONS:

29

A REVISED CONCEPT OF GOD

I run in the path of your commands, for you have set my heart free.

Psalm 119:32 (TNIV)

I adjusted my recliner to a suitable angle and reached for my steaming cup of coffee. No sound broke the silence except the steady tick tock of the wall clock. Winter sun streamed through east-facing windows, creating warmth on my arm and spreading light in the room. Peace and contentment filled my heart and mind.

My thoughts drifted back over the decades, back to the child who formed her first ideas about God. Thousands of encounters and experiences had brought me to the evolution of my knowledge of the Triune God. The essential characteristics I developed then had not changed—merely my interpretation of them.

A God Who Rescues

From my childish "escape from consequences" view of God, I progressed to a deeper understanding of how God rescues me when I look to Him for help. There have been many times when I have cried out, "Lord, I've landed myself in a jam. I know you're gracious and merciful. Please bail me out of this, show me what to do." As time passed, I came to the astounding realization that God is able to bring good out of anything.

What I thought was a devastating blow to my happiness turned out to be one of God's greatest kindnesses. Knowing all I now know about my childhood development, I am grateful I was somehow prevented from embarking on what would have been a disastrous marriage. Worse, I might have unwittingly inflicted emotional damage on children.

My singleness, however, meant more than escape from dire circumstances. It gave me freedom to block out all distractions and single-mindedly pursue my quest. It also afforded me the golden opportunity to begin exploring the life of my mind, to unearth buried talents and abilities.

Either state, married or single, has plusses and minuses. In my case, God took what I considered a huge minus and taught me how to turn it into a significant plus.

A God of Expectations

The image of a God who constantly raised the performance bar faded. In its place is the picture of a trusted mentor—a wise teacher or counselor, someone who desires the best *for* me and *of* me. Greatest of all, this is someone who has known me from conception. It's always comforting to meet up with a person I've known all my life, to enjoy the unspoken bond between us. Since I'm an immigrant, this doesn't happen often, so I value it even more.

I have transferred this thinking to my concept of God. He appointed Jesus, the Master Teacher, to instruct me, to give me a vision of what I could become through His power working in me. He has high expectations of me and delights in seeing positive changes. God's ultimate expectation is that I be conformed to the image of Jesus, although I can't see this happening until I get to heaven!

A God Who Provides

I changed my "get from God" thinking to an implicit trust that "*God gives the best to those who leave the choice to Him.*" I present my dreams, desires, and requests with open hands, an open mind, and the prayer that God in His wisdom will overrule and prevent me from pushing through any door He is trying to close. When I pray simply for either green lights to move forward or red lights to stop in my tracks, I am astounded to discover that this works.

I experience financial provision—and split-second timing—beyond coincidence. Panic still looms because of money challenges, but then I recall an enormously consoling example of God's planning. The manna the Israelites ate in the wilderness did not cease until *the day after* they ate some of the produce of their new homeland.[85] There are no gaps in God's supply—and my daily "manna" keeps coming.

Such overwhelming care and provision prompts a "give to God" attitude. He is worthy of my love, worship, and service.

A God Who Sees and Hears

In my daily prayer time, I thank God for His protection, provision, and preservation—but most of all, His presence. I draw comfort from the fact He is supremely attentive, that I have Jesus' assurance he will never leave me, nor forsake me. I can rest in the knowledge that whatever circumstance may come my way is filtered through fingers of love. It comes clothed in purpose, for my growth or the good of others.

A God Who Helps

From frantic pleas for help at exam times, I progressed through petitions for wisdom and guidance in my career, financial decisions, relationships, relocation, and travel.

Then I discovered an unanticipated aspect of God's help—encouragement to become the person He designed me to be. He engineered my circumstances and placed my feet on a path that resurrected long-buried creativity.

A God Who Heals

I continue to be "alone" by societal standards, yet I enjoy a deep sense of belonging that has little to do with my physical circumstances. Emotional healing is the greatest miracle of all. While the scars of past hurts remain, the gaping void is filled.

Jesus really does have a stupendous back loader.

A God of Obligations

God is still a God of obligations, but to my delight, I discovered the obligation is *toward* me, not solely expected *from* me. He has made promises in His Word and is obligated to keep them, despite my confusion, sense of impending doom, or any other volatile emotion. This awareness is like a rock on a slippery path, or a firm branch to grasp while I regain my balance. I choose by my will to believe that God will honor His word and that Jesus, through the Spirit, will hold me steady on this often treacherous road called life on Earth.

A God to Be Obeyed

God still expected obedience. My study of the Israelites' journey made this abundantly clear. Yahweh meant what He said. However, He was not the "Heavenly Policeman" of my childhood, ready to pounce on me for the least infraction. I had looked beyond the law of the commandments to the character of the One who wrote the law, and examined the reasoning behind the rules. They were given in love for my good—not to inhibit my happiness.

He outlined Skill for Living guidelines. By following these, I could expect protection (or a bail-out) from foolish mistakes. I have secure parameters—and the freedom to move at will within those parameters. The One calling for obedience is not some capricious authority figure. He gives me the opportunity to connect with the manufacturer's blueprint for life as a human.

My will has become God-directed.

A Distant God

. . . who drew near, who loved me enough to send Jesus into the world to experience and understand the limitations of the astoundingly complex creatures He had created.

Not only did Jesus provide a link to the Father and an example, but of crucial importance, he learned the challenges of exercising free will. Understanding this makes Jesus' experience of facing Satan's attempts in the wilderness to allure and derail his purpose, plus his struggle in the Garden of Gethsemane, achingly real. He could have said "yes" to the former and "no" to the latter.

I turn to the Greatest Counselor in times of uncertainty or confusion and know with assurance that the Spirit will guide. He infuses a sense of stability in my inner being I never thought possible.

A New Purpose in Living

I have read countless books about the will of God—what it is, what God expects of me, how to find His will, the importance of doing His will, and the dire consequences of failing to do so. Confusion and fear over making a mistake and missing out on God's "perfect will" had immobilized me in the past. My time in Wisdom School brought me to the realization that God has two distinct purposes for His children.

The **Doing** purpose involves fulfilling whatever task God assigns. At the mere mention of "God's will," people automatically think of missionaries in some foreign country. Or certainly the term conjures up images of involvement in some aspect of ministry. But a creative God has an infinite variety of opportunities, outlets, and avenues of service. He makes sure the task is custom-designed for the unique abilities He has already given and the training He is more than willing to provide. I make myself available; He chooses how best to use me to accomplish His purposes.

Of much greater importance is the **Being** purpose. The Westminster catechism states that our primary aspiration should be to "love God and enjoy Him forever." This involves simply enjoying being God's child, bringing Him pleasure by trust and confidence in His goodness and care. As I allow Christ to live in and through me, I become a mirror of who he is, giving an accurate reflection to those around me.

I am free to be who I am and as God made me, His unique child.

I am free to do what He assigns me. "I delight to do Your will, O my God; yes, Your law is within my heart."[86]

With immense relief I acknowledge I am also free to fail. Any formula that prevents failure also prevents freedom. But fear of failure, of not measuring up, no longer drives my behavior. Lloyd John Ogilvie uses the analogy of a plumb line—a means of measuring whether something is straight or crooked. Jesus is God's plumb line. Each day I ask that he make me aware of anything in my life that is out of plumb. And he does!

Addressing God

The question of how to address God in my prayers puzzled me for some time. I hear people referring to

Almighty God, Heavenly Father, Lord Jesus, or the Spirit, generally one or the other. I developed my own descriptive way of addressing the triune God:

God Above and Around Me:

Almighty God, sovereign ruler of the universe, the great "I AM," the God who goes ahead and makes things happen,

Gracious and loving, kind, generous, attentive *Abba* (Papa),

God Next to Me:

Lord Jesus, my savior, lover, companion, healer, advocate, defender, deliverer, shepherd,

God In Me:

Holy Spirit, my strength, sustainer, power, inspiration, instructor, guide, counselor, stability, comforter, nurturer,

O LORD, my Lord . . .

Thank you that I can take time out to meet with you. Thank you that in your omniscience you know everything about my circumstances.

I pray that you will reveal yourself to me today, make me aware of your love and all that you desire to be to me at this time.

In your graciousness and compassion, will you act on my behalf as I present these specific needs to you, trusting in your character, your faithfulness, and your wisdom . . .

This introduction reminds me of the all-encompassing sufficiency of God. It doesn't matter what my struggle *du jour* may be, at least one characteristic from my list covers my need. I also find it helps to repeat these traits when I question their validity. I know God is kind and generous, even when He appears not to be. I know the Spirit will guide even when I seem to be floundering or spinning my wheels. I know Jesus' power to heal, restore, deliver is as effectual as it was when he walked on Earth.

I added an ending to my daily prayer that encapsulates my new way of thinking:

> And now, Lord, I commit this day to you. Will you give me today what you see I need for the day; nudge me along in the direction you want me to go.
> I pray above all that Christ may be formed in me, and that your power will continue to work in me to will and to act according to your good pleasure and purpose.
> Amen.

Pointer: The Creator of the Universe is Infinitely Creative

- Are you ready for the adventure of a lifetime? Challenges that will stretch you to your limits? Interventions that will leave you speechless?

- Relax and enjoy the process as the invisible God continues to teach you about Himself and demonstrates His desire to be involved in your life.

- You will be amazed at all Jesus offers and the creative, intensely personal ways in which the Spirit communicates.

Count on this! God is utterly trustworthy.

POINTER REFLECTIONS:

30

FINDING JOY

. . . I carried you on eagles' wings and brought you to myself.

Exodus 19:4 (TNIV)

Many years have passed since the day I sat on top of Mount Sinai and wondered what it might be like to know God one-on-one as Moses did, to have an open, honest, intimate relationship with Him. All I understood at the time were my feelings of being bound by the trappings of religion and the frustration of my efforts to please a distant God. I was clueless as to the deeper psychological issues cemented into the core of my being.

My journey through the "wilderness" took many twists and turns. I wandered into dead ends. Deep ravines and high mountains blocked my path, necessitating that I find a way around or tunnel through. Flash floods of unexpected emotions sent me tumbling, spinning upside down and leaving me gasping. The hot sun of adversity beat down mercilessly, sapping my meager strength. I trudged along, impelled by the hunger and thirst of my unfulfilled needs, hoping that the shimmer ahead would turn out to be an oasis and not a mirage.

Yet as I wandered, I tasted the free life. I felt the wind on my face, the exhilaration of the dry desert air. I exulted in the triumph of slaying "giants," one after the other. I was freed from the constraints of someone else's views. I experienced the relief of unexpected provision, the mysterious security of the awareness of an overshadowing, guiding hand. I savored the incomprehensible knowledge that my Creator wanted an intimate relationship with me! I discovered aspects of God's character that surprised and delighted me. My vision was broadened, my understanding deepened. My immature, self-centered concept of God evaporated like early dew in the bright rays of the sun as I came to appreciate who He truly is.

I learned the lessons embedded in the story of the Exodus, the essence of what God wanted to convey to His creation:

> There is only one true God.
> He is a God who comes near to His children and makes Himself known.
> He has a purpose for each life and wants to make it known.
> He is active in the world He has made and in the lives of His children.
> He is God of the past, the present, and the future—unchanging and unchangeable.

I uncovered what was, to me, a far more significant revelation of God's purpose than the mere event of leading the people on their historic journey to a land of their own. The words of Leviticus 26:12 tap into the artesian well of God's amazing love and care for humans:

> I am the LORD your God, who brought you
> out of Egypt so that you would no longer
> be slaves to the Egyptians; I broke the bars
> of your yoke and enabled you to *walk with
> heads held high*" (italics mine).

God worked internally while He dealt externally with His people.

In discarding religion, I discovered reality, the reality of authentic faith in an undeniably real God. I tossed out the rulebook handed down to me and stepped off the performance treadmill. The tightly coiled spring of insecurity and fear at my core slowly released. No longer do I constantly peer into the future, trying to find the next visible marker along the path (although this remains a temptation). I am learning to trust the character of the God who asks me to trust Him.

God works from the inside out, not from the outside in. As in the model of the equal-arm balance, the power runs from the source, the Triune God. My pan of *Self* is never static. I am changing, growing, being reshaped through my connection to the power source.

The crossbar of my will controls the flow, directing the energy toward *Others* or *Self* in response to the prompting of the Spirit. The result is a scale in balance, the picture of a wholly integrated human being: spiritual, relational, psychological.

I am profoundly grateful that God did not answer my prayer to win the Reader's Digest Sweepstakes. His plan was infinitely superior to mine. I do not need unlimited material blessings. What I need is the daily assurance that the invisible God is there, He is aware, and He cares. His mysterious and serendipitous interventions in my circumstances astound me and mean far more than mere financial security. With certainty I can assert that God gave me the best because I left the choice to Him.

I never had a spectacular supernatural encounter with God. I never heard His audible voice, saw Jesus, nor an angel. Yet, in answer to my original question, "Does Christianity work?" I can now declare, "Absolutely!" It works in a far different and infinitely better manner from what I originally thought.

How does it work? I have no idea.

But then I cannot figure out how a signal from a satellite overhead bounces off the receiver perched on the corner of my house and turns it into a picture on my television. I still find faxes spooky.

The Creator of the universe established the laws of gravity, physics, and aerodynamics, and I believe these operate even when I don't understand them. The mighty God who put these laws in place says the Christ of Christianity is able to enter my spirit when I invite Him in. I accept He can do just as He said. Belief is a matter of the will.

My daring gamble paid off, far beyond anything I could ever have imagined.

A Hero Before Moses

Abraham in the Old Testament was the "test pilot" of the life of trusting an invisible God. He learned his lessons well. Abraham is revered as the father of the Israelites and was later honored with the title "Friend of God."

Eugene Peterson gives a superb description of this new lifestyle of freedom. It hangs in front of my computer, where every day I read:

> (Abraham) lived by faith. He was living in response to God, obeying God, consulting God, being changed by God, being challenged by God, growing in relationship to God, listening to God, praising God, believing God.
>
> Did Abraham have a twenty-year plan with carefully defined objectives as he launched his important career as father of the faithful? No, there were delays, interruptions, detours, failures. He didn't do it all correctly—he didn't live without doubt or sin or despair—but he did it. He followed and confessed and prayed and believed. God was alive for him. God was the center for him.[*]

I'd like to have these words said about me some day. I cannot think of a more worthy tribute. God was the support column of Abraham's life. Amazingly, He has become my support column.

---

[*]Eugene H. Peterson, *Traveling Light*, Colorado Springs, CO: Helmers & Howard, 1988, p. 102. Used by permission.

I am Equipped! I am Adequate! I am Loved!

This morning I woke up, stretched, and lay quietly thinking. As I contemplated a new day, the rays of an invisible sun broke into my mind. Warmth spread through me, expanding into the farthest recesses of my being. A deep sense of peace and contentment spoke the message that whatever the day held, I was equipped to handle it.

My support column remained enduringly solid. I could draw on available resources in my relationships. I had a power source to help compensate for personal deficiencies. The shackles of religious programming were dropping away. I enjoy a sense of bubbling freedom that makes me want to run, spread my arms, and twirl. The words of the Psalmist David captured my newfound feeling, "I run in the path of your commands, for you have set my heart free."

What an amazing plan! All-encompassing, timeless, enduring. It inspired me to add one more phrase to my daily prayer: "May my acceptance and enjoyment of your love, my trust in your character and your word, my confidence in your faithfulness bring you pleasure today."

When I get to wherever God takes His children when they die, I will fall on my knees in wonder and gratitude to thank such an awesome God for His great heart of love that made its fulfillment possible.

Then I want a big hug from Jesus and to hear him say, with feeling, "Well done, Joy, you are a Super Conqueror."

Later I will seek out Moses, heartily shake his hand, and say, "Thank you, Moses, for pointing me in the right direction."

After that I will try to find some of those ancient Israelites. I'd like to thank them for the hope and encouragement I found through the record of their struggles to learn to trust an invisible God.

POINTER: The Journey Continues . . .

Thank you for journeying alongside me through this book. I pray your heart and mind will have been opened to the magnificence of the invisible God who went to such great lengths to draw His ultimate creation back into relationship with Him.

POINTER REFLECTIONS:

REFERENCES

[1] Psalm 84:11
[2] Psalm 27:13 (NASB)
[3] Numbers 6:24-26 (KJV)
[4] Proverbs 3:5, 6 (KJV)
[5] Zechariah 4:6 (KJV)
[6] Matthew 6:33 (KJV)
[7] Colin Whittaker, *Seven Pentecostal Pioneers*, Basingstoke, U.K.: Marshalls Paperbacks, 1983, p. 48
[8] Ibid., 19
[9] Luke 10:4
[10] Acts 4:34, 35
[11] Hebrews 13:8
[12] Whittaker, 76
[13] John H. Dobson, *A Guide to Exodus*, Judson Press, 1978, p. 47
[14] *The New Bible Commentary Revised*, Ed. D. Guthrie, J.A. Motyer, A.M. Stibbs, D.J. Wiseman, London: Inter-Varsity Press, 1970, p. 126
[15] Exodus 14:11, 12 (NASB)
[16] Exodus 14:13 (NASB)
[17] Exodus 31:18
[18] Matthew 22:37-39 (NASB)
[19] W. E. Vine, *Vine's Expository Dictionary of Old and New Testament Words*, Old Tappan, New Jersey: Fleming H. Revel Company, 1981, p. 207
[20] Ibid., 54
[21] Hebrews 11:6
[22] St. Augustine of Hippo, *On The Trinity*, Book I, Chap. I
[23] Colossians 1:15
[24] John 14:6
[25] Lloyd John Ogilvie, *The Bush is Still Burning*, Waco, Texas: Word, Incorporated, 1980
[26] John 15

27   Galatians 5:22
28   Revelation 3:20
29   A.W. Tozer, *Man: The Dwelling Place of God*, Harrisburg, Penn.: Christian Publications.
30   Exodus 19:8
31   Psalm 84:11
32   Robert Robinson, "Come, Thou Fount"
33   Numbers 14:1-4 (TLB)
34   Numbers 14:7-9 (TLB)
35   John 14:14
36   Proverbs 16:33
37   Hosea 2:14, 15
38   Romans 12:2 (AMP)
39   Robert H. Schuller, *Putting Your Faith Into Action Today!* Robert H. Schuller, 1983, 1990
40   Psalm 27:13 (NASB)
41   Habakkuk 3:17, 18
42   Matthew 6
43   Numbers 10:33
44   Numbers 11:4-6
45   John 14:20, 21 (NASB)
46   Nehemiah 13:30
47   Proverbs 1:7 (NASB)
48   *The New Open Bible* Study Edition, Nashville, Tenn.: Thomas Nelson Publishers, 1990, p. 701
49   John 18:37
50   Acts 17:11
51   David Johnson & Jeff VanVonderen, *The Subtle Power of Spiritual Abuse*, Minneapolis, MN: Bethany House Publishers, 1991, pp. 113, 114
52   Ibid., p. 16
53   Jude 1:4
54   Psalm 131:2 (NASB)
55   Matthew 16:24 (KJV)
56   Romans 7:14-24

57   Galatians 6:3 (KJV)

58   Hebrews 12:1-2

59   Jay E. Adams, "Nouthetic Counseling is Not New," The National Association of Nouthetic Counselors, www.NANC.org. Accessed January 2003.

60   Hebrews 13:8

61   Adams, "Nouthetic Counseling is Not New"

62   Matthew 22:39

63   Matthew 5:18

64   Psalm 103:14

65   Ephesians 3:16-20

66   Matthew 21:21

67   1 Corinthians 12:9

68   Philippians 2:13 (AMP)

69   Isaiah 42:16

70   Richard L. Flournoy, Ph.D., Frank B. Minirth, M.D., Paul D. Meier, M.D., States V. Skipper, Ph.D., *100 Ways to Obtain Peace*, Grand Rapids, Mich.: Baker Book House, 1985, p. 26

71   John 10:3, 4

72   Flournoy, et al, p. 48

73   Numbers 23:19

74   Joel 2:25 (NASB)

75   Galatians 2:20 (AMP)

76   Job 42: 5, 6

77   Job 42:16, 17

78   Isaiah 55:8, 9

79   2 Timothy 1:7

80   2 Corinthians 10:4, 5

81   Ephesians 6:10, 11, 13

82   George Keith, "A Firm Foundation"

83   Romans 8:28, 31, 37

84   Ephesians 3:20 (AMP)

85   Joshua 5:12

86   Psalm 40:8 (AMP)